The Monochrome Of Darkness

The Journey of a Fallen Angel
Vol. 1

Channing H. McClaren

Table of Contents

- Cover Page
- Table Of Contents
- Introduction
- Prologue
- Journey of a Fallen Angel
- Final Cover before the Verses.
- Untitled

Introduction

My heartfelt encomium for downloading my ebook. The book revolves around my selected set of verses which I have handpicked from my collective journals.

Thank you for choosing to read.

Channing McClaren

Channing H. McClaren

Prologue

This volume of writing is an elegy to my soul, it's my deepest darkest intonations of mind, that I have researched over and over within my soul to pen.

Times write tales on the palms of epiphanies, perhaps it carved on mine one such, a deep dark line that resurrected time and time again in my inks. I have wavered beneath the ashes of my own resurrections. I have seen torments, hell wouldn't desire. I have basked in the sunlight of love and I have been doomed under it.

I am the waves of an ocean, the glimmering shine over the rustles. I am the winds of storms; I have dazzled my days in search of curses.

I used to think I was a writer, a poet. In the crevices between many heartaches, my dark eyes now finally see. A light that leads to darkness, perhaps I am darkest of poets, perhaps I am nothing.

But...

I think I resonate in many memories, sometimes as an ink, sometimes as a love as a cure and sometimes as a curse.

Something I am inking again and the winds took away.

-Channing

Vol. 1

THE MONOCHROME OF DARKNESS

My journey of verses begins....

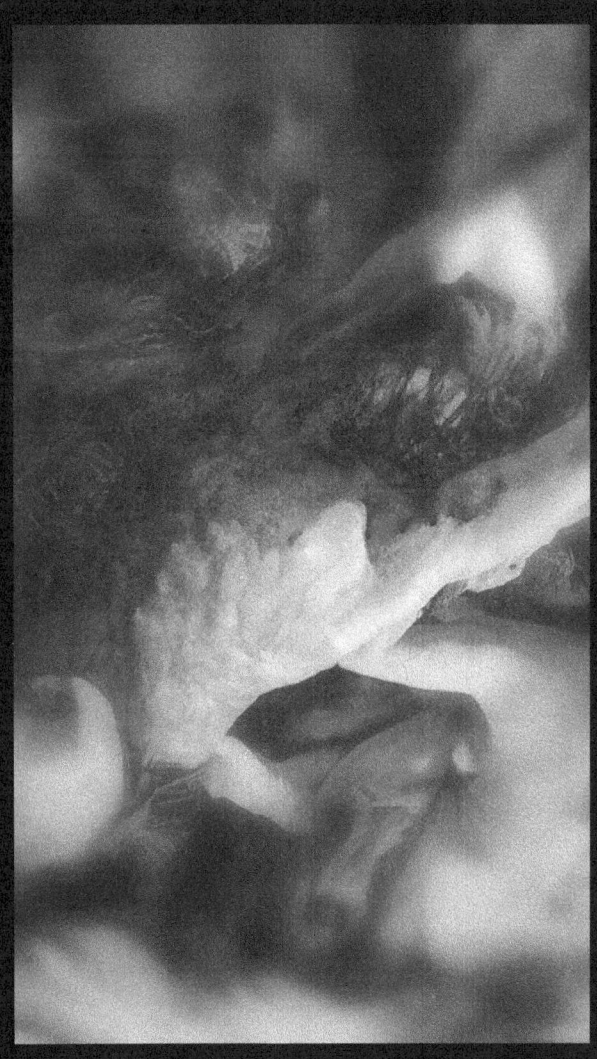

Journey of a Fallen Angel

"I was a wound they said, a wound which bled even a rose. A wound that lusted a thorn from a pricked skin. I was a massacre...

of frond, of fogged lakes...

I was shunned from ideation; cautioned as death."

~ Channing M, The Monochrome of Darkness

Journey of a Fallen Angel

"The shadows have breathed me in, it has made a galore out of my breaths.

I inhale its scent, venomous and tinted, I am its hemisphere... I am it's lost asset.

Who has scythed such a ferocious illness inside me? Such a decayment of horror I became?

Graveyards under Graveyards that my body has buried itself in."

~ Channing M, The Monochrome of Darkness

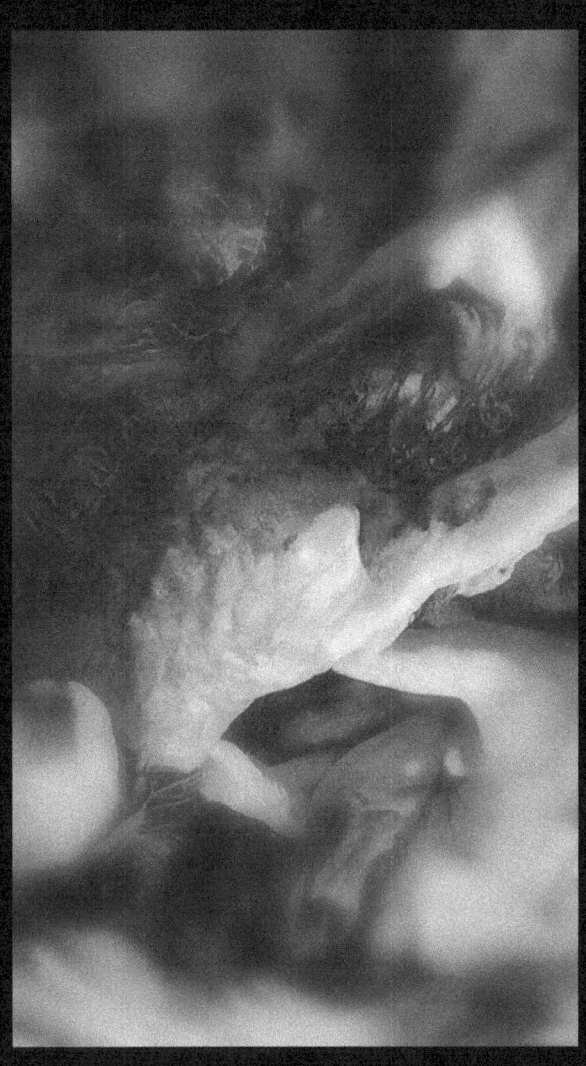

Journey of a Fallen Angel

"That black ore of the natural order, pining the hands of a ghost...

lost asunder under the wicked dark lavender vines, melted in thirst —

of decay, of disharmony, of blacken shapes...

of which I am a shadow... molded in crimson dark shroud."

~ Channing M, The Monochrome of Darkness

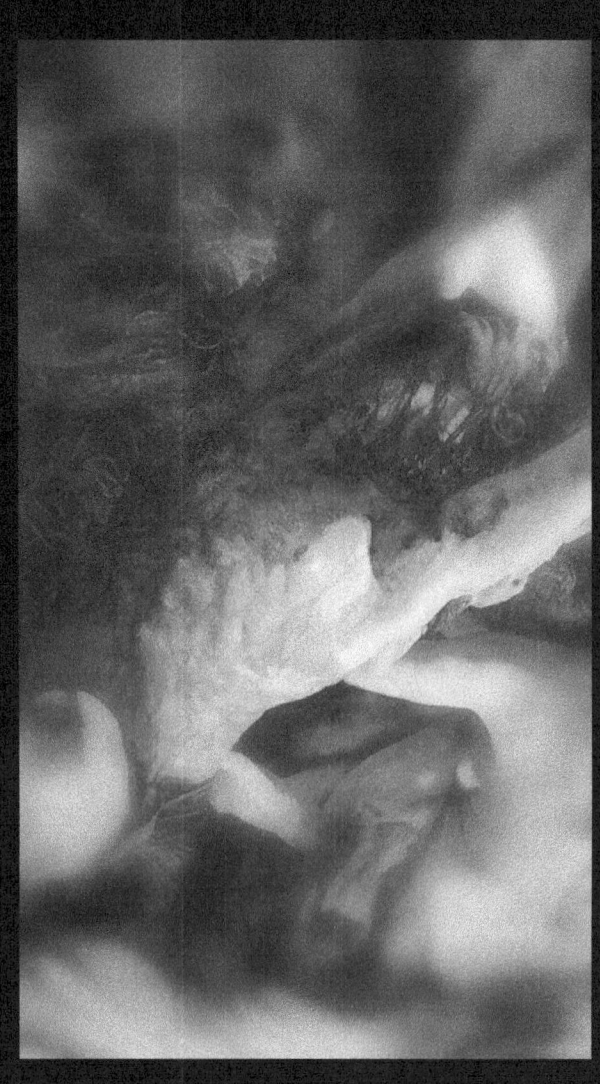

Journey of a Fallen Angel

"Six of crows, offed at my bloodless door,

the sultry shadows of the light, my veins? how daringly had forgotten to fight.

For lustrous the shadows of evenings were, in compass, in heart in beneath the door....

for this languid laid at her door of death...

be coffined, bloodless, soulless the wade.

I am a harp, I thought, the string of which had been broken or was I the string of the Harp?

irreparable for existence..."

~ Channing M, The Monochrome of Darkness

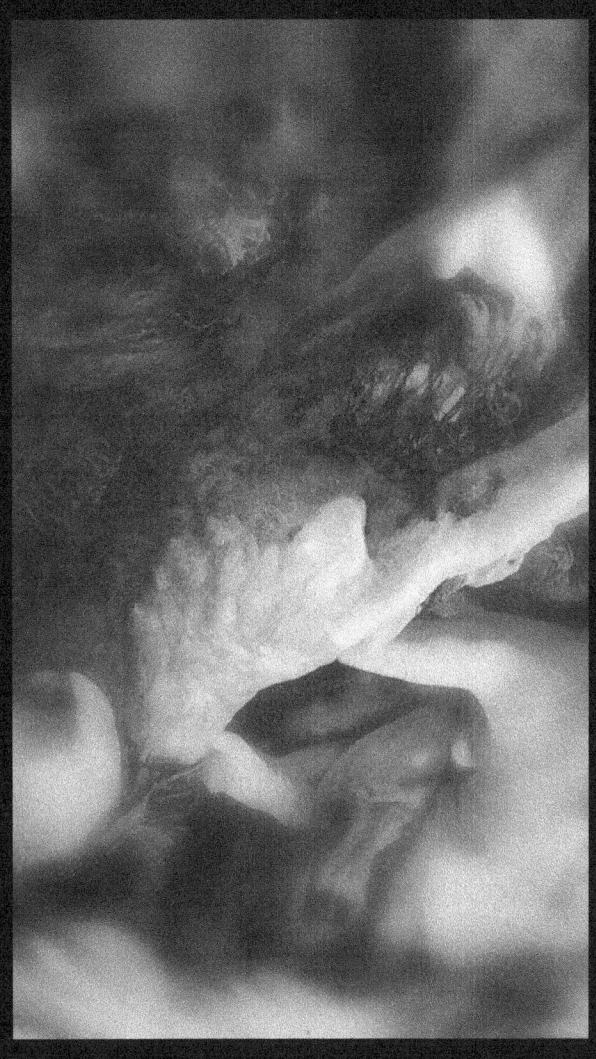

Journey of a Fallen Angel

"I only hear birds now — quavering underneath the broken Opera, and I am that ghost — a colophon of a snake...

lustrous, powerful, broken, dead."

~ Channing M. The Monochrome of Darkness

Journey of a Fallen Angel

"A lynch? A chant? A verb? What effect do the weathers cause? Within what darkness A Star Is Born? In what light it tends to decay and die?

Yes, a lynch I would call it. Every time, I have looked out of that ivy laden window...

I have seen a ghost hanging, with a noose around its' neck in an enchantment of salvation."

~ Channing M. The Monochrome of Darkness

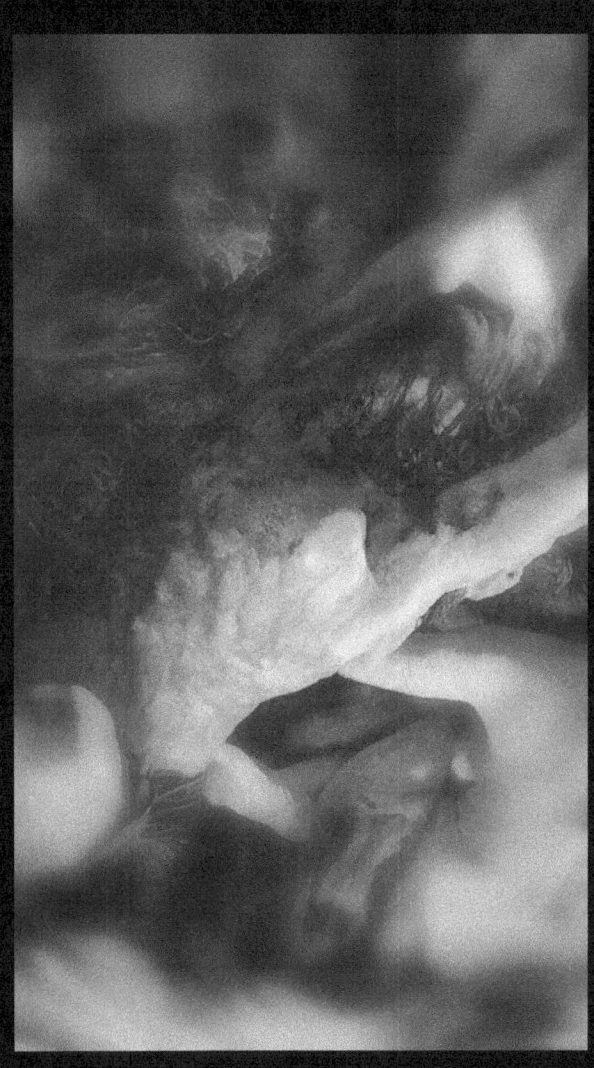

Journey of a Fallen Angel

"I am the vicar of old tombs, bleeding toxic chants in the name of Praise."

~ Channing M. The Monochrome of Darkness

Journey of a Fallen Angel

"Warped, the snake moved ashore—
that poisonous murder of a dint,
inside which I breathed a hymn,
losing my skin..."

~ Channing M. The Monochrome of Darkness

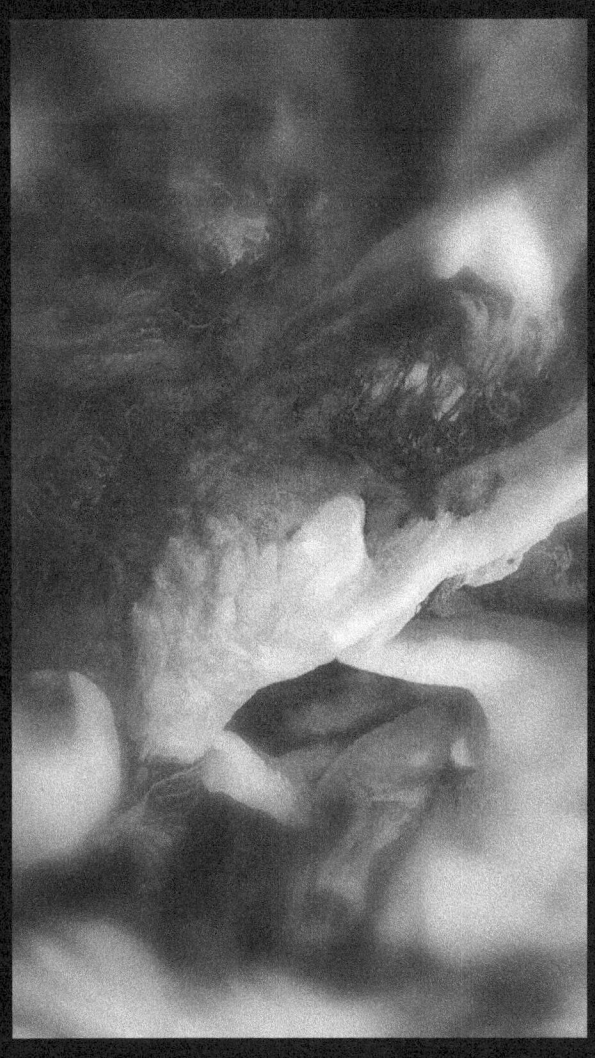

Journey of a Fallen Angel

"And how many horror stories I ask, were born out of love?

Of ghosts screeching for touch, for the arms of a love forsaken,

abandoned in storms, left to rot."

~ Channing M, The Monochrome of Darkness

Journey of a Fallen Angel

"I was untouchable like a ghost who roamed with white hair and shaken memories.

I did not know why I had become so starved of love that I chose to even reject it.

: The very starvation, The very need.

Like a Ghost to me everything was impaired.

Everything looked as if through a lens of wanting to find the light, wanting to die even as a Ghost..."

~Channing M. The Monochrome of Darkness

Journey of a Fallen Angel

"My wicked lonely wings of the night, as if have become impaired with a sorrow of darkest light;

I am a corona, a bleeding inscribe. A taste that venom has lost, an effluvium of the sigh.

Exasperating for breaths gone from life.

What coffins could shade a ghost? That marred, that broken, of immortal shame in essence, of the mortal coil, maiming the air of the night."

~ Channing M, The Monochrome of Darkness

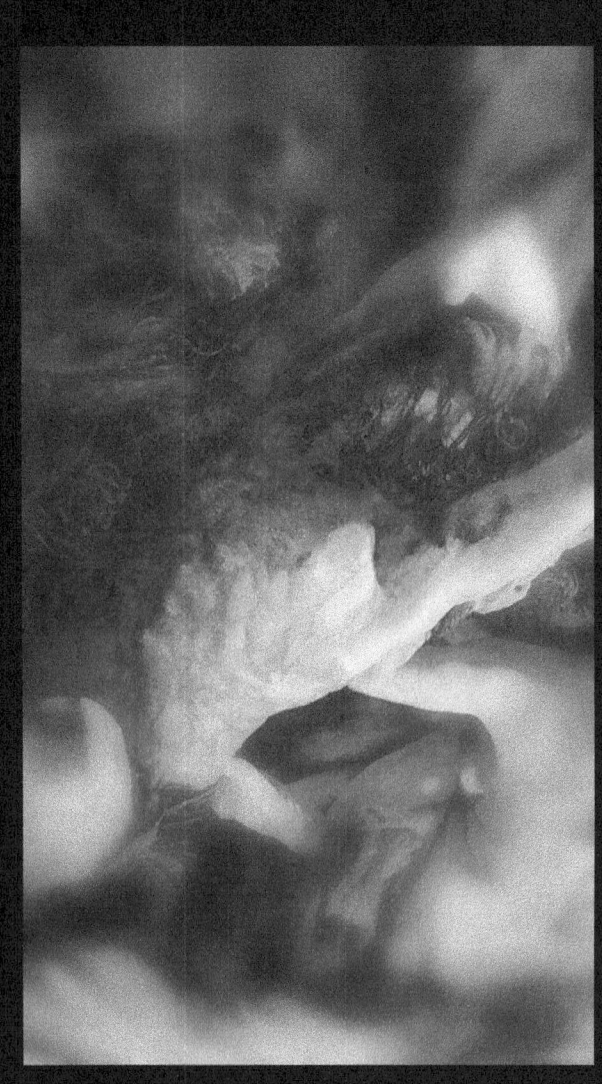

"Ink, the blood dropping ink, writing from my veins, I have lost a link to say how perilous, shallow the world has become and I, it's distant ache..."

~ Channing M. The Monochrome of Darkness

Journey of a Fallen Angel

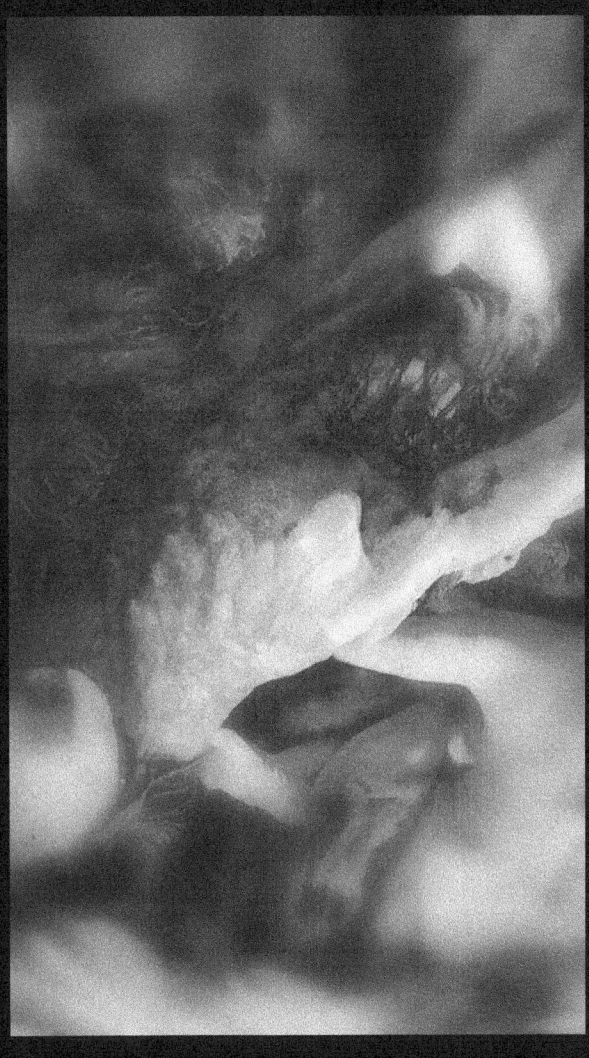

Journey of a Fallen Angel

"Do dead creatures feel pain I appetizingly ask, Is the blood a mere wound or is the mind a wound stuck on an unfounded blood?"

~ Channing M. The Monochrome of Darkness

Journey of a Fallen Angel

"My heart is torn between the two, the death and the living, as if the mortuary mixes the paint on the canvas of living death, a harbinger of my making, a portrait of its own spell."

~ Channing M, The Monochrome of Darkness

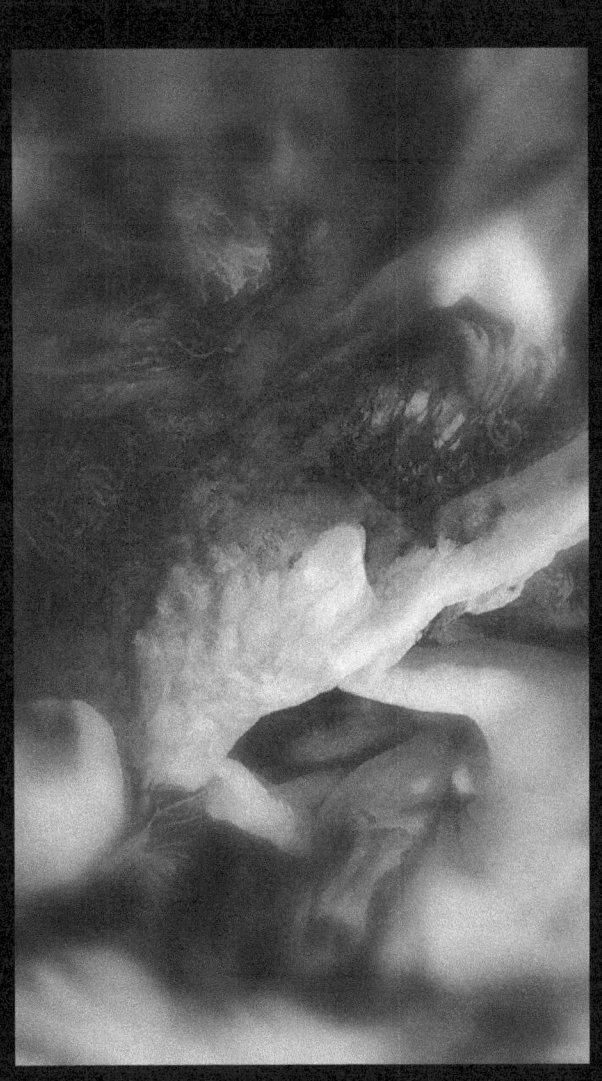

Journey of a Fallen Angel

"I am a chain of ashes, smitten by death; procreated in chaos. No rhythm can hold me, I am dead through a pair of living eyes. I am insanity in a grain of sand."

~ Channing M. The Monochrome of Darkness

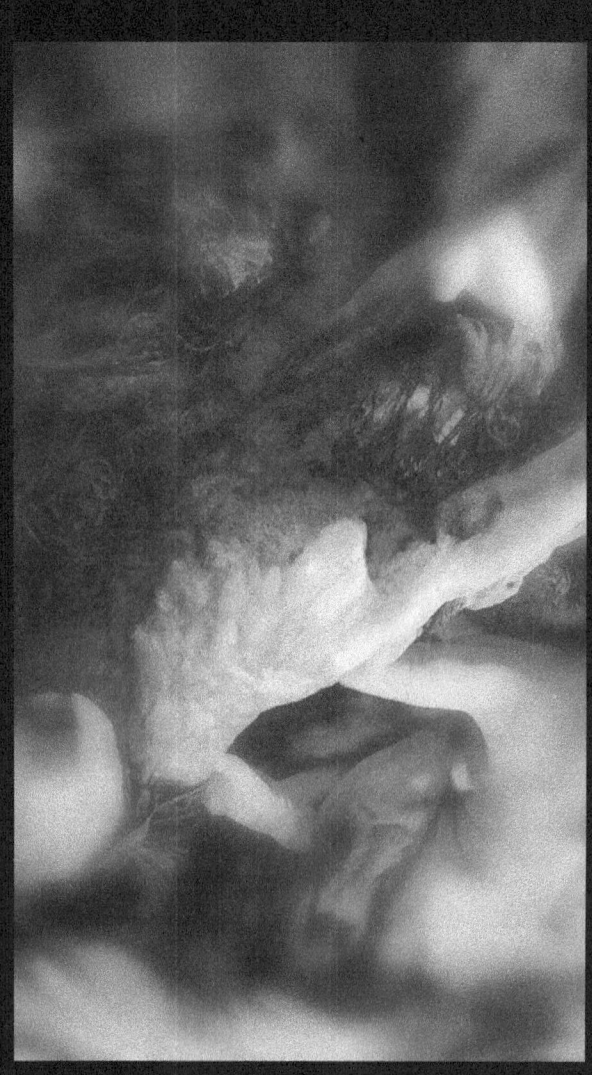

Journey of a Fallen Angel

"I am slow-burning dread, tired, timeless and poisonous..."

~ Channing M, The Monochrome of Darkness

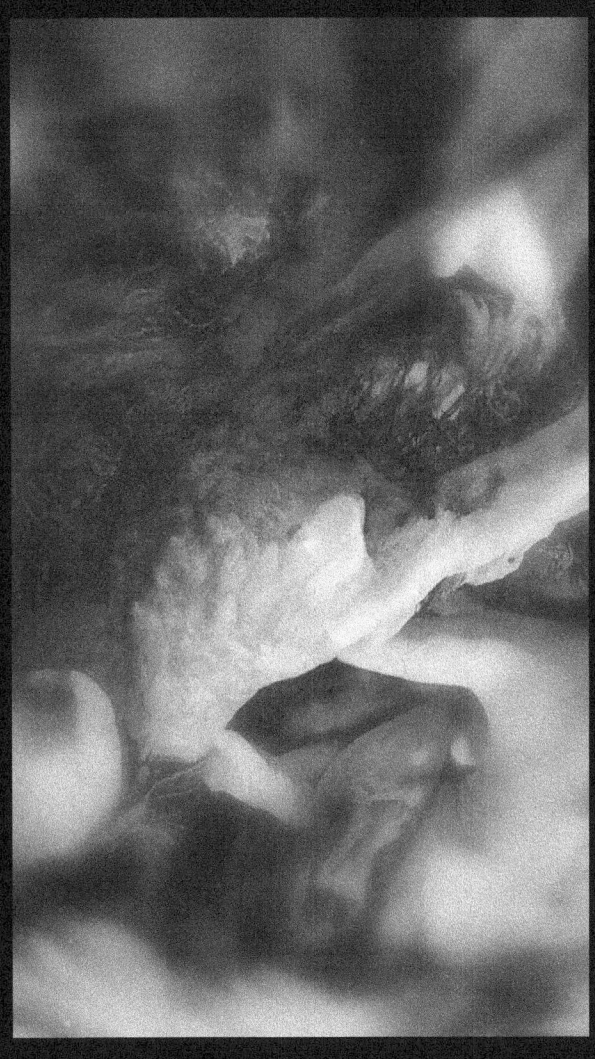

Journey of a Fallen Angel

"I demand wars to martyr me, in quiet that only birds can hear... am I a blasphemy of a saint who used to be? Like a dead man who has lost his tale? or am I the sun setting ashes of death incarnate?"

~ Channing M, The Monochrome of Darkness

Journey of a Fallen Angel

"Writhe my heart, wound my knee, I hold the mist in the palms of my hand as though a realm forsaken, in which I lived a fogged existence.

I am marred and derailed; I am the tears of lamented skies, my blood has frozen in demise of my heart.

I am the wound of an ancient sorrow..."

~ Channing M, The Monochrome of Darkness.

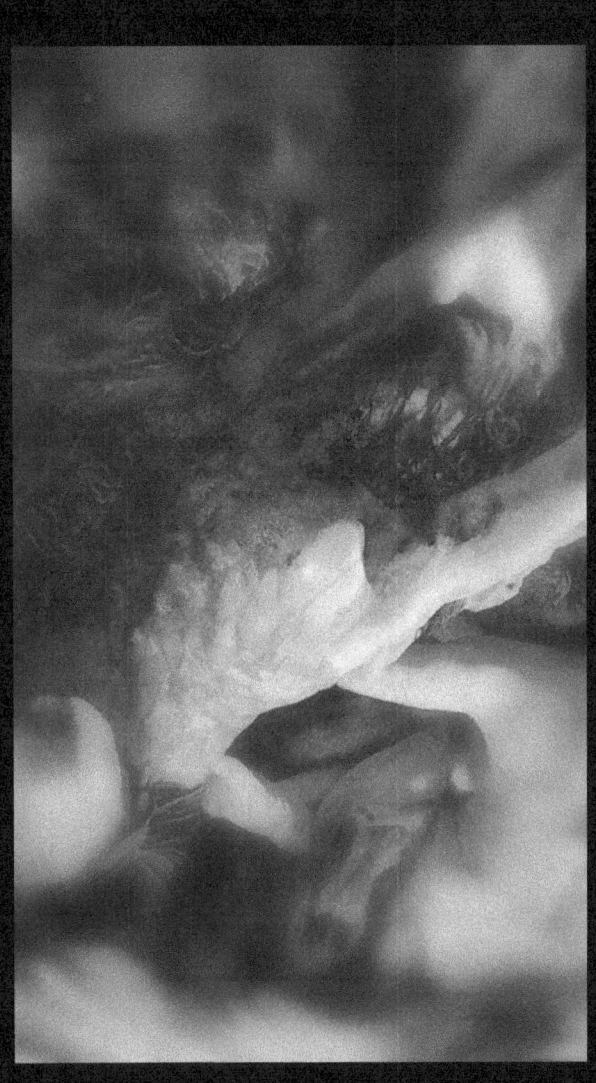

Journey of a Fallen Angel

"How? Tell me... How to face the dead while being alive? How to walk through the mirror through your breaths? How to live Kingly in ghastly under shades while being alive? How to get smudged in the echo of the night, still breathing? The death demands a price.."

~ Channing M, The Monochrome of Darkness

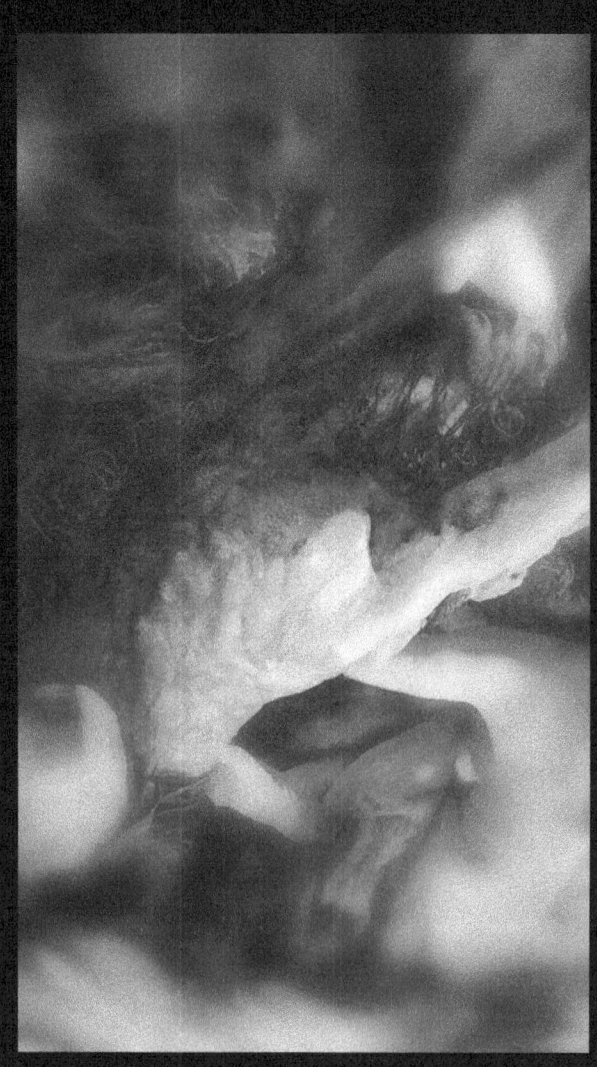

Journey of a Fallen Angel

"Through midnight I tread, into a land of moratorium... Where the dead speak of life, and the living speak of dead. With an adder at heart, I tread with ambrosial water of life, feeding the dead a skin of death; painting the virulence, etching the blood in my eyes."

~ Channing M. The Monochrome of Darkness

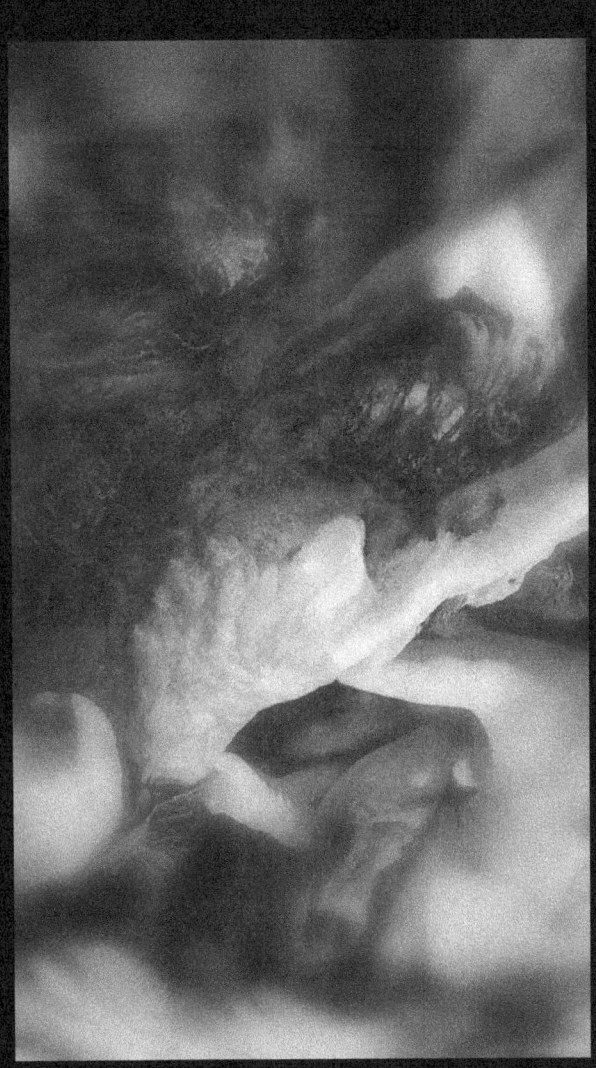

Journey of a Fallen Angel

"My words are possessed, spirited, ghosted; they haunt my skin, like a snake hissing at murder."

~ Channing M, The Monochrome of Darkness

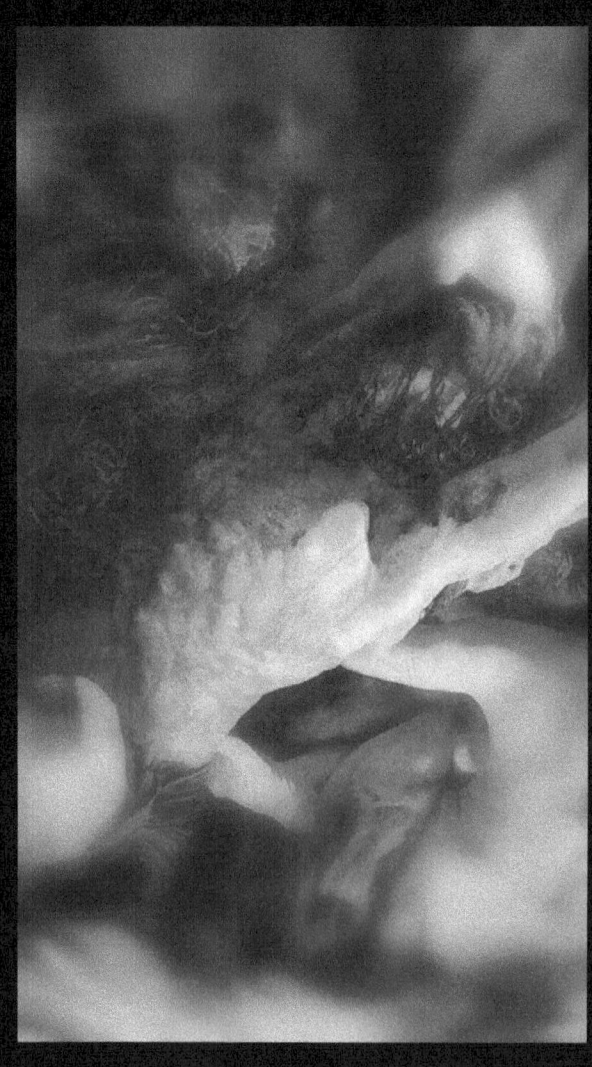

Journey of a Fallen Angel

"Looked akin wayward, a sailor full of impaled gaze; a star that broken off of his compass, a tear saved. For what skies must he look upon on a storm lit night? A penny. A lover, or a mysterious delight. Looking back at a nuptial saved on his finger made for ring: love, heart, desire, saved in a skin. That shores that wash him off from his tremulous sin, am I he? The sailor? or the storm killing him.."

~ Channing M, The Monochrome Of Darkness

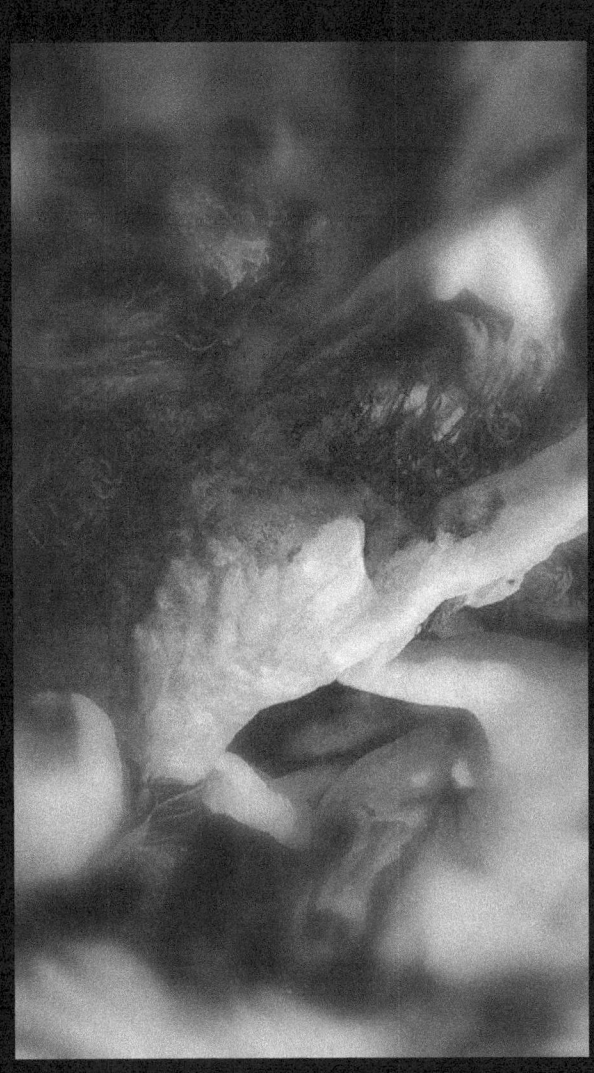

"I am an ocean full of roses, darkening at the edge of a sunset."

~ Channing M. The Monochrome of Darkness

Journey of a Fallen Angel

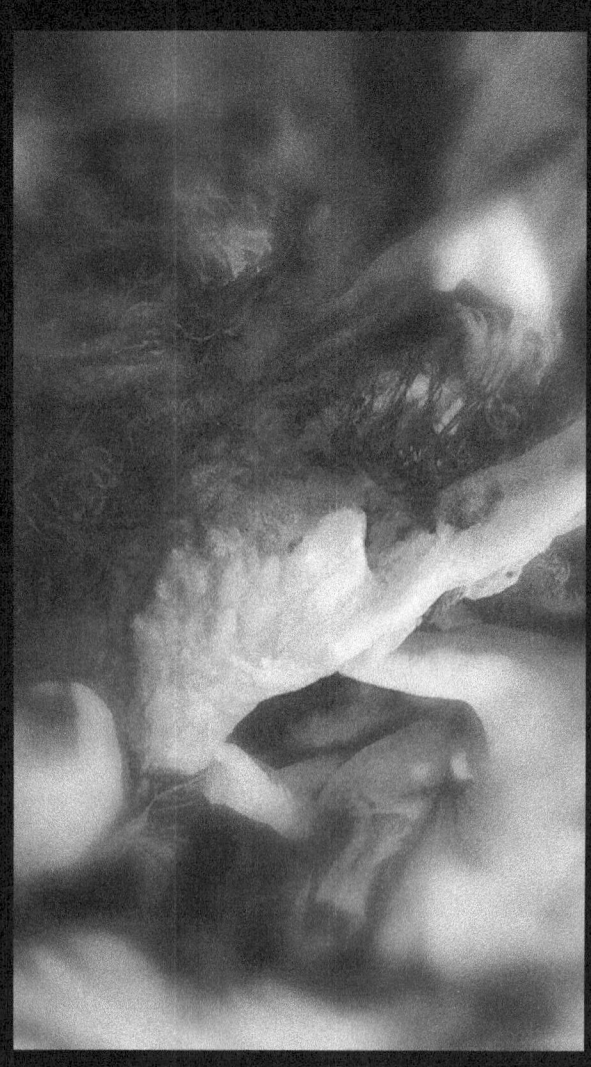

Journey of a Fallen Angel

"I became a mortification of a portrait that started to speak,

as beautiful the exterior was painted, the more I rotted within...
Dripping blood from the contours of it, as if dying to express a truth hidden, which had to be lived, but just by the portrait alone..
withering, my eyes, losing the efface, the blemishes...
I was a portrait that could speak, of love, of death and of horrendous insanity, of hysteria, of aberration."

~ Channing M, The Monochrome of Darkness.

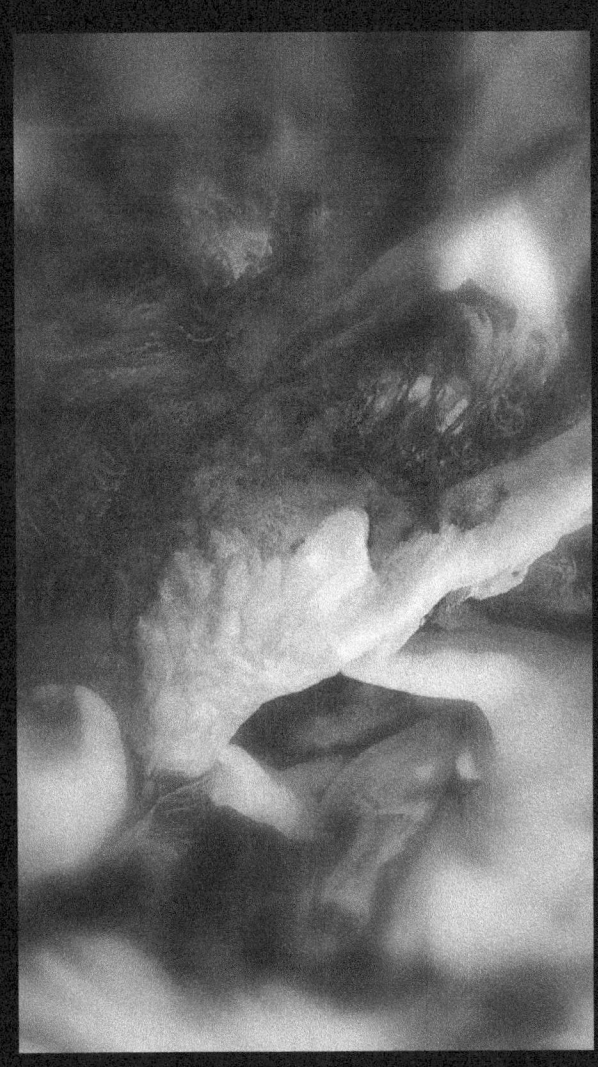

Journey of a Fallen Angel

"Hang my flesh on the branches of willows.

Let it drip of howls of forlorn ghosts. Let the scowling winds wash away the painful scars from my flesh.

Let the ghosts reap an abandonment

From what skies have I fallen?

In a dearth full of death and decayment?

Is my voice that covered with a shroud, lamenting blood? or am I just a frozen ache of a distressed widow."

~ Channing M. The Monochrome of Darkness

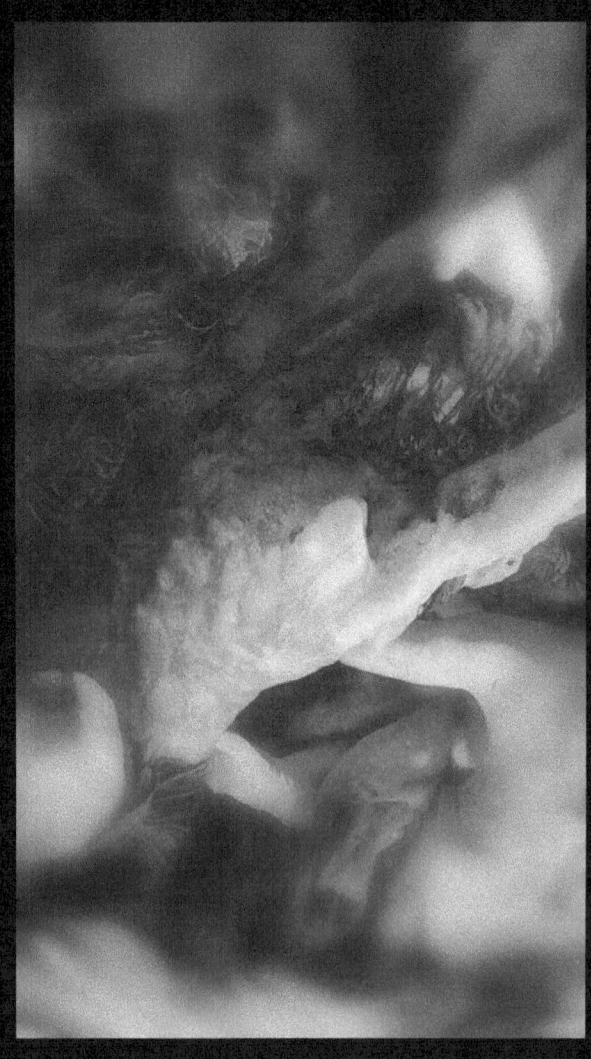

Journey of a Fallen Angel

"Wavering skies falter underneath a shadowed gloom, crevassing blood screeched tales, ghosted at the edge of bottomless pits, tales stitched in darkness, tales perched on a hooted olive branch in ghastly winter, the mood, that downtrodden from the walks of rotting flesh, reeking of ghosts seeking refuge..."

~ Channing M, The Monochrome of Darkness

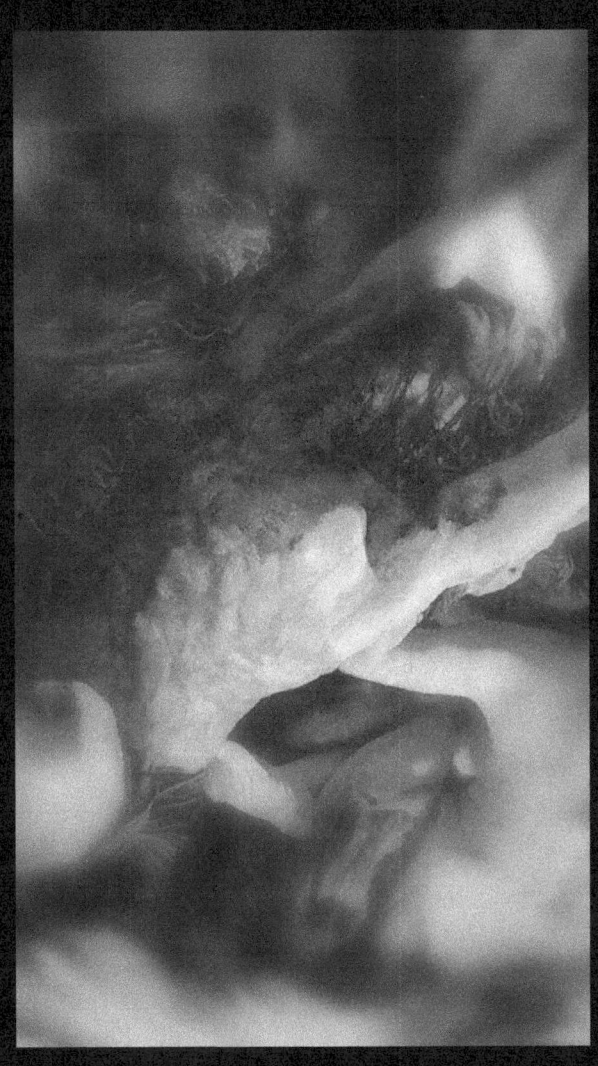

Journey of a Fallen Angel

"Woe is me who in a trance-like wake, sleeps under the ashlar of wicked past ghosts. I that waned, like a flicking candle fanning in winds of escape. Maiming to die."

~ Channing M. The Monochrome of Darkness

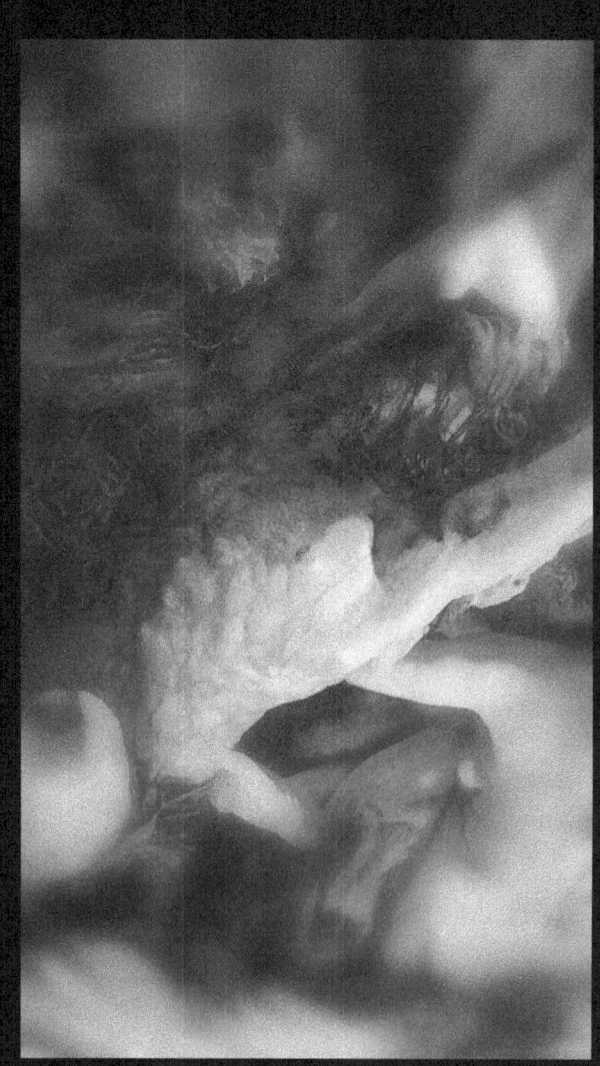

Journey of a Fallen Angel

"The most terrifying horror I expose is that with every passing facade; every feeling — tear, emotion, love, loneliness; has become in my eyes — absolutely nothing."

~ Channing M, The Monochrome of Darkness

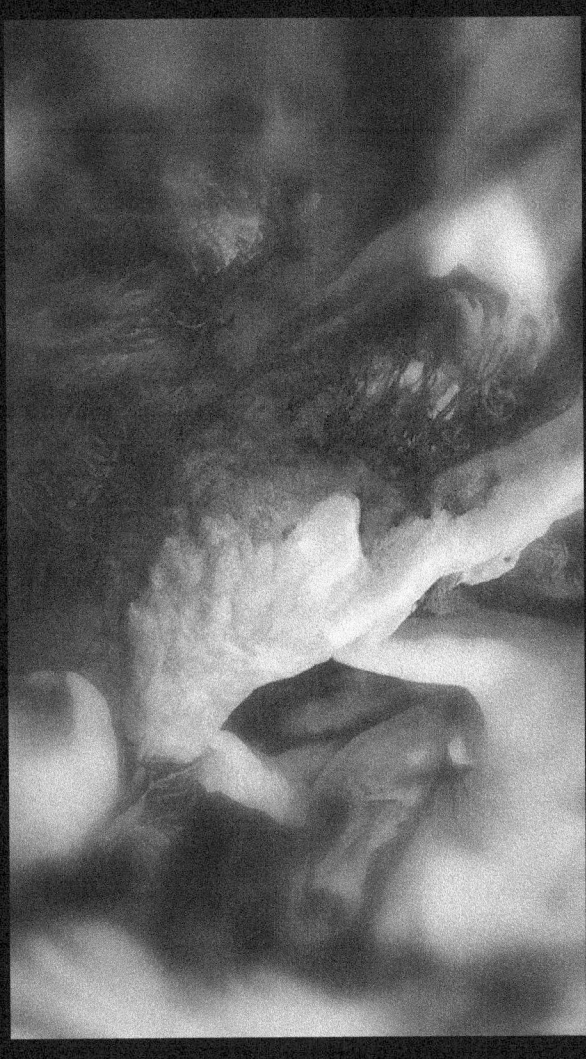

Journey of a Fallen Angel

"What I am, is war...
An ache of crystallized deceit, of revolutions combined, in one flesh. What I am is war...
The continuity of which the wretched hours seem to shun. A cosmic darkness that senses paralyze. What am I? If not a war of a thousand demons combined in a God."

~ Channing M. The Monochrome of Darkness

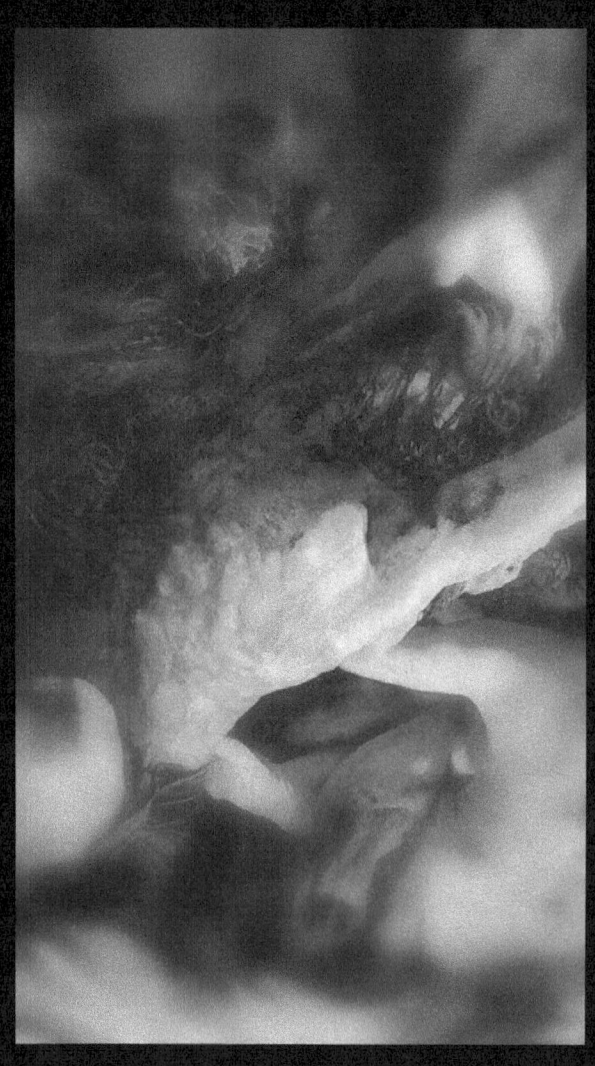

Journey of a Fallen Angel

"Have you ever seen the world from dead eyes? Things in shape and forms of ghosts? Painting Octobers with red moons as autumns with death? What of the broken twig hanging from the branch in early November? Are the ghosts too angry? Too cold and weak to leave traces, but only enough? The fog that laments... is now suddenly numb? Scaping mists with crimson. Have you ever seen the world from dead eyes?"

~ Channing M. The Monochrome of Darkness

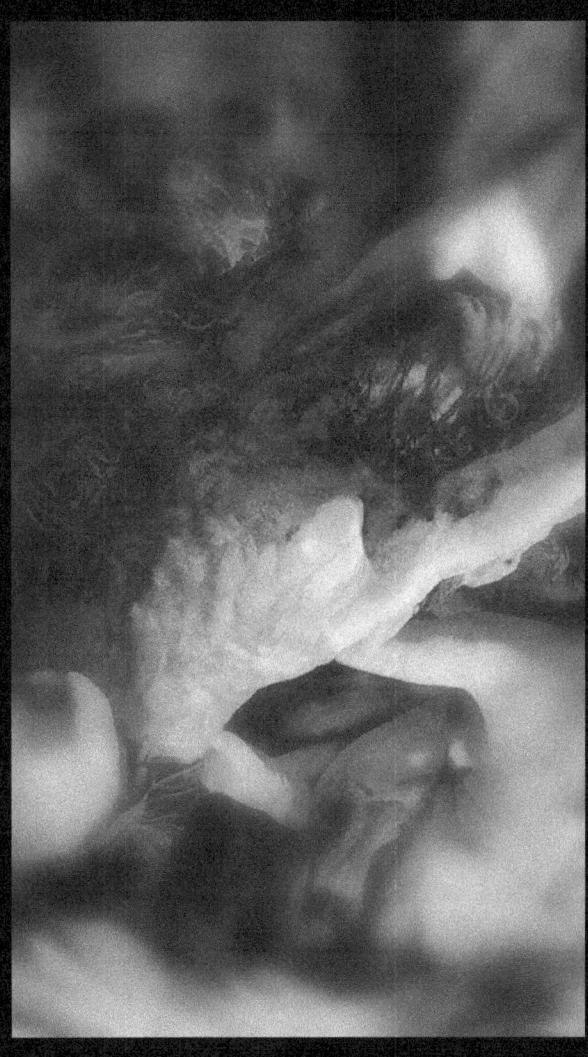

Journey of a Fallen Angel

"the dark phases of the moon, slay his Stygian soul, the darkest pits, hanging over, ruinous- like the stained blood blotting on the sheets of skies... my eyes that asunder, looking forth towards the east of a dead dawn...

my tears fracturing the nights of hell."

~ Channing M, The Monochrome Of Darkness

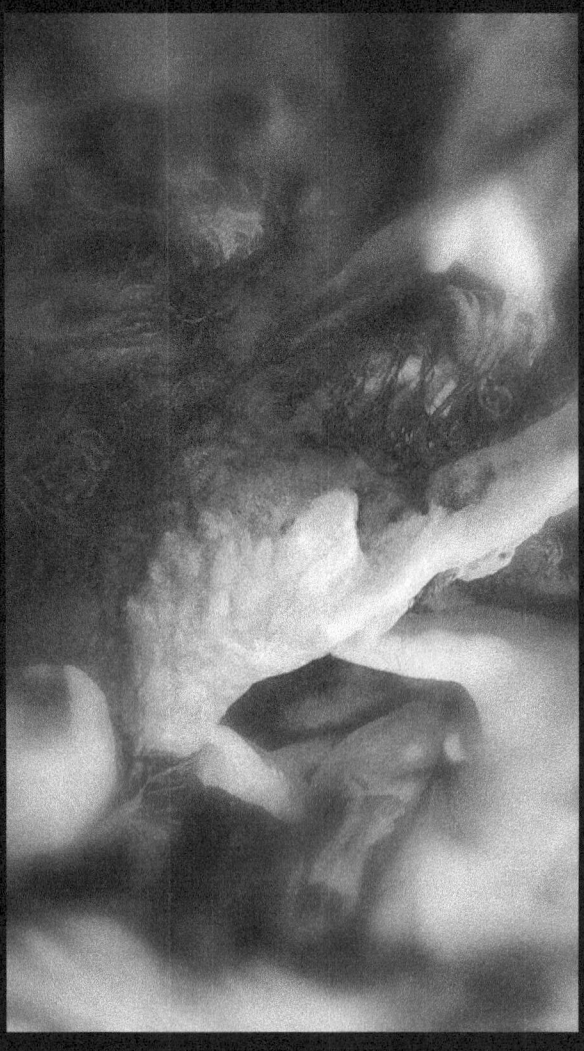

Journey of a Fallen Angel

"I have applauded the mist in the eyes of my lover, that decays even incontinence, even severe senility...
There she says it was 'only you'... as if I lack the passionate lust of the stroke of death...
What then, her eyes construe, with such beguiling vision on the curvatures of my palm...
I have been such a death of a muscle that has atrophied from lack of use...
I am he that beautiful and dead...
I am the darkened unchanging portrait of myself..."

~ Channing M, The Monochrome of Darkness

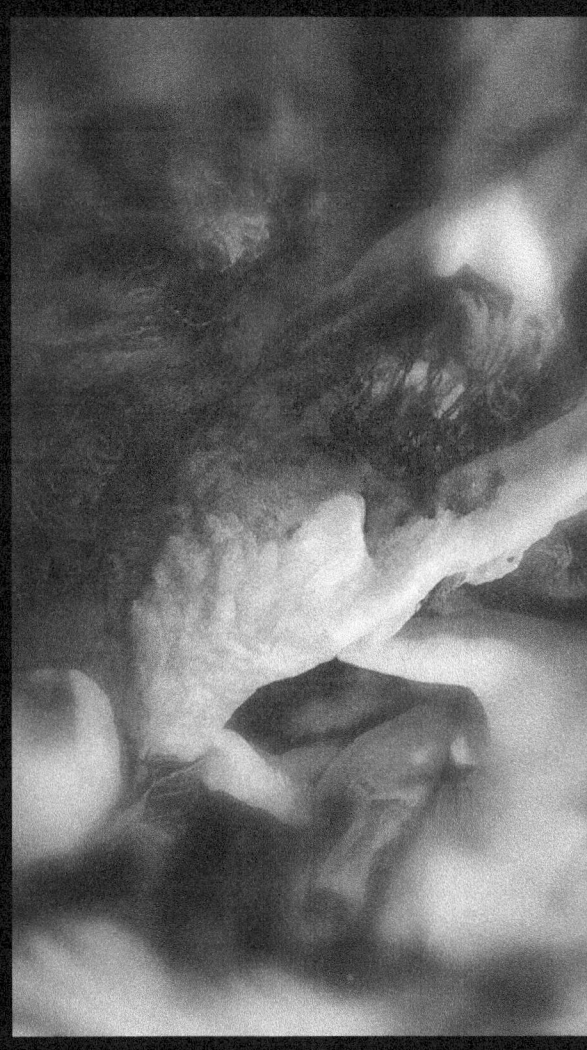

Journey of a Fallen Angel

"The method groaning in his madness, a wandering pollute his eyes sets out to be, naught like a woe is he, a dissonance asserts, wielding dark fogged mirrors across his lamenting flesh, this arcade of ever-growing numbness, these Cathedrals of solace, now averts a dire repentance of bleeding cobwebs and heartless whispers. He is a fantasy of a demonic sky heavily panting at night."

~ Channing M, The Monochrome of Darkness

Journey of a Fallen Angel

"He kissed a crowned abyss, the expires of his wailing, wasted in air... like three twisted tears from hell, gauzing the head of the beast."

~ Channing M, The Monochrome of Darkness

Journey of a Fallen Angel

"I am a heartless beast, the blood on my Canine is a wound. The bleeding ashes of my soul, that softly merge in the scent of the air, asks for parting from a corded Ghost."

~ Channing M, The Monochrome of Darkness

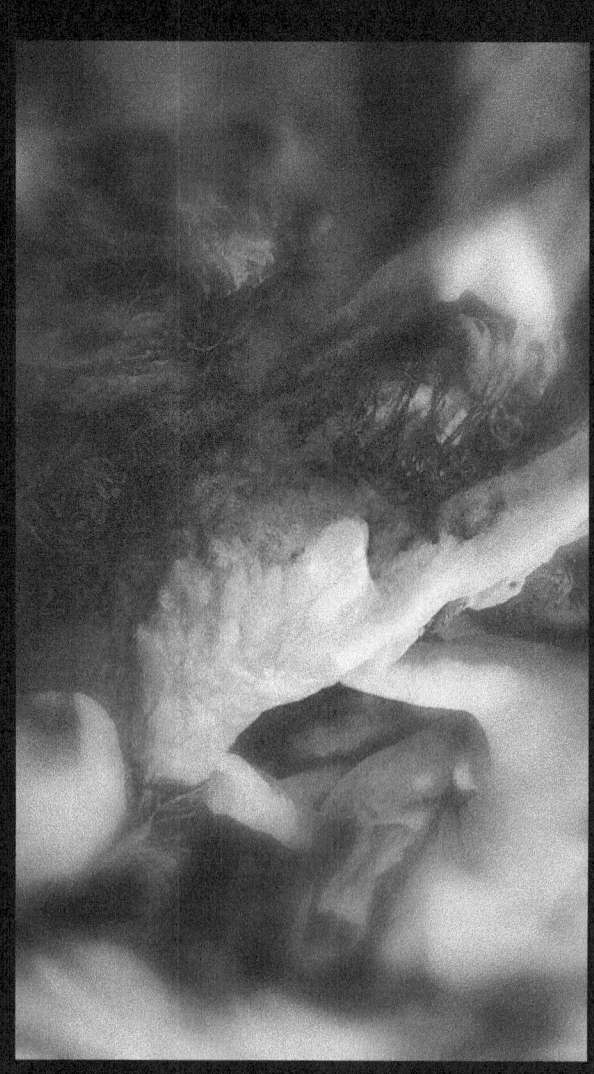

Journey of a Fallen Angel

"He walks on infernal waters, untouched like a ghost, like a white shadow that has lost the verve to shelter his own shroud."

~ Channing M, The Monochrome of Darkness

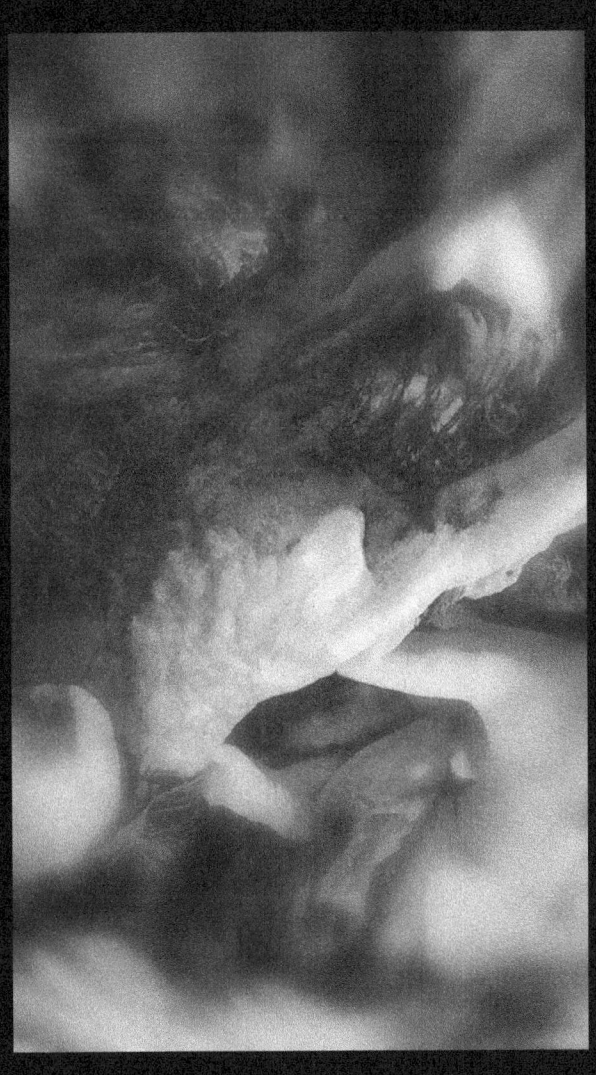

Journey of a Fallen Angel

"Often these words that shrieking and galactic, my whispers come to seek, the ocean filled drownage of its consonance, in a murderous vessel of my mind, slow as I am to find them, start lamenting in a hooting groan. My eyes, that foreseeable of a coming storm."

~ Channing M. The Monochrome of Darkness

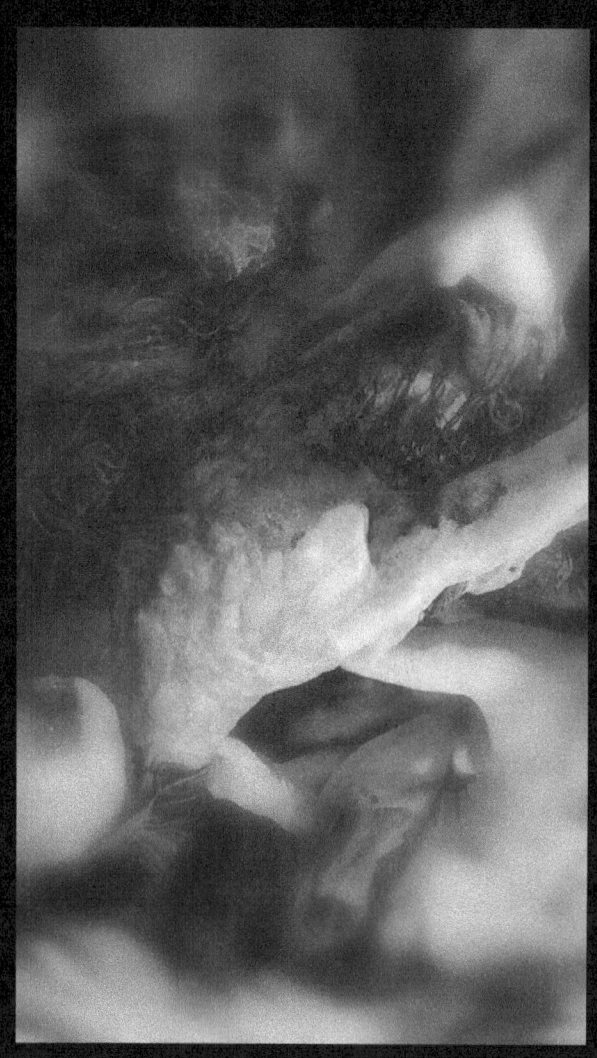

Journey of a Fallen Angel

"Languid lies in this sultry strain. Benighted, howling, marred in his pain. For hours of decay wander through his pale skin; Frosted and dismissed on the rainy ground. Abject grey eyes travel, of his, from meandering woods to coffins of the slain."

~ Channing M. The Monochrome of Darkness

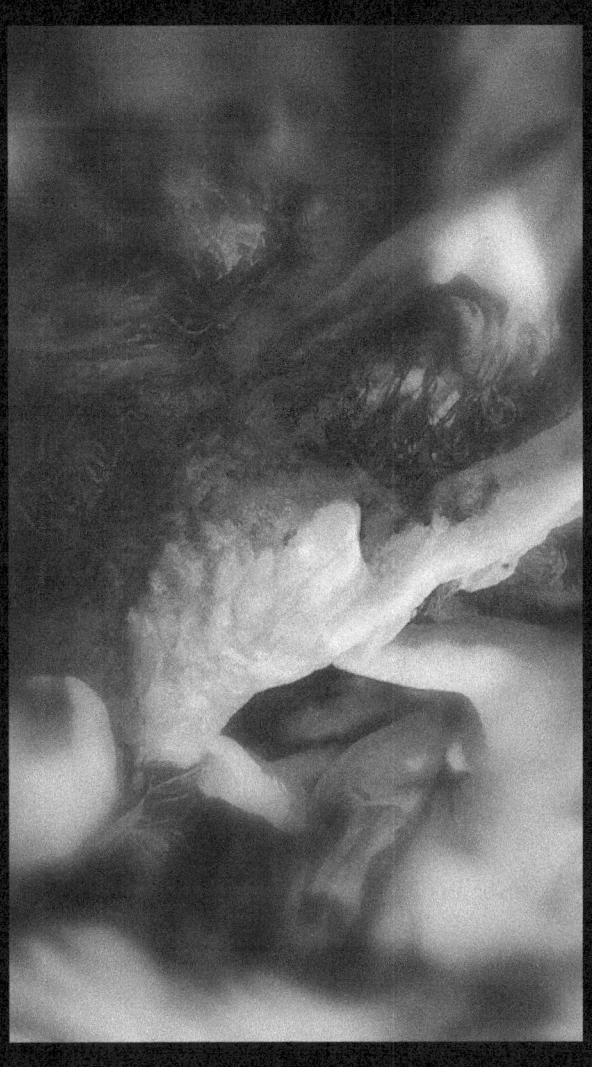

Journey of a Fallen Angel

"This night has painted me in colours of flames and ashes. I am a cauldron of wounds tonight, garnering blood from the sparks my veins infuse; I am a scream, I am a call of death, I am a pendulum of madness: An incarceration of mayhem."

~ Channing M, The Monochrome of Darkness

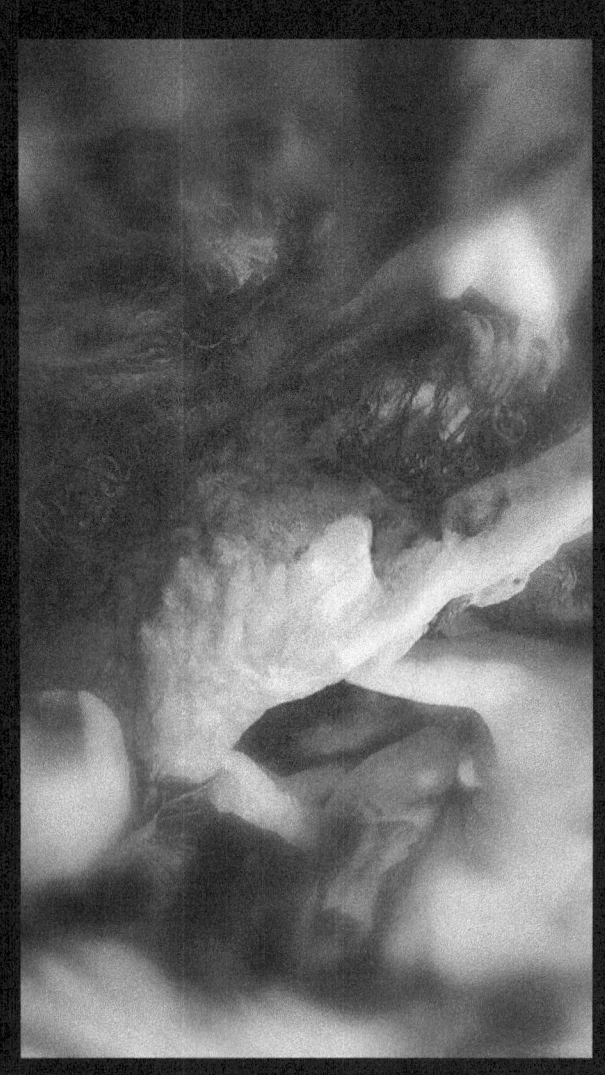

Journey of a Fallen Angel

"I cannot be equaled let alone bettered at the edge of your thoughts, that like a voracious snake I would poison sibilating my rage on your withered stares."

~ Channing M. The Monochrome of Darkness

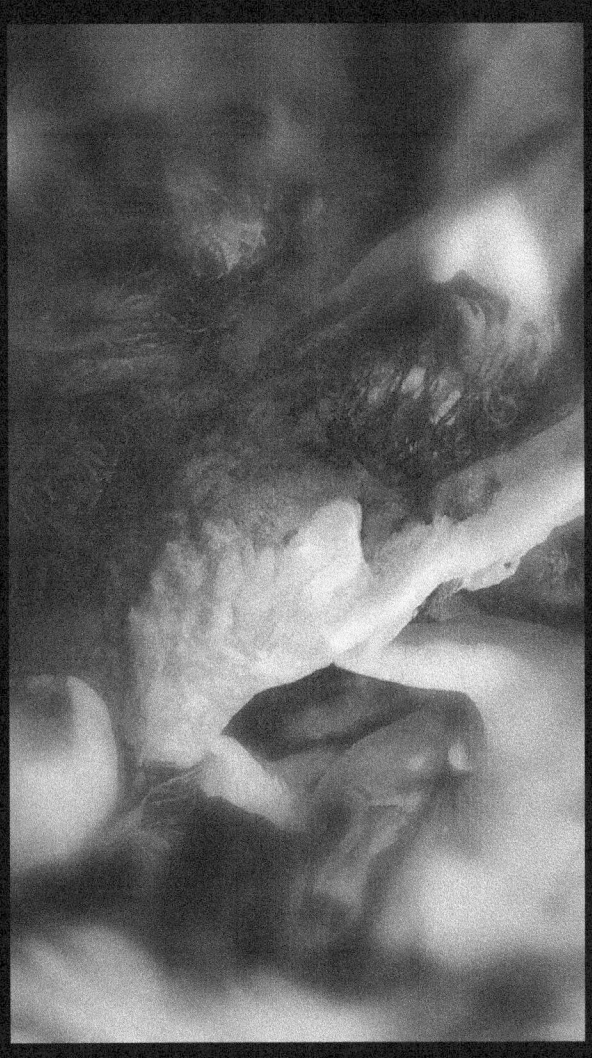

Journey of a Fallen Angel

"Visage lies underneath Kings of Ruins, coiled snakes hissing for sin, in random black temples of South, where winds frantically fear breeding, for hark! my heart that red brooding... the springs bleeding autumns in palms of moon or breaths garnering the lament within. Bleed my heart of ancient cries, Sorrows compeer my veiled eyes. The sea that swallows my birds of night, I am a reverie in the heart of a demise."

~ Channing M, The Monochrome of Darkness

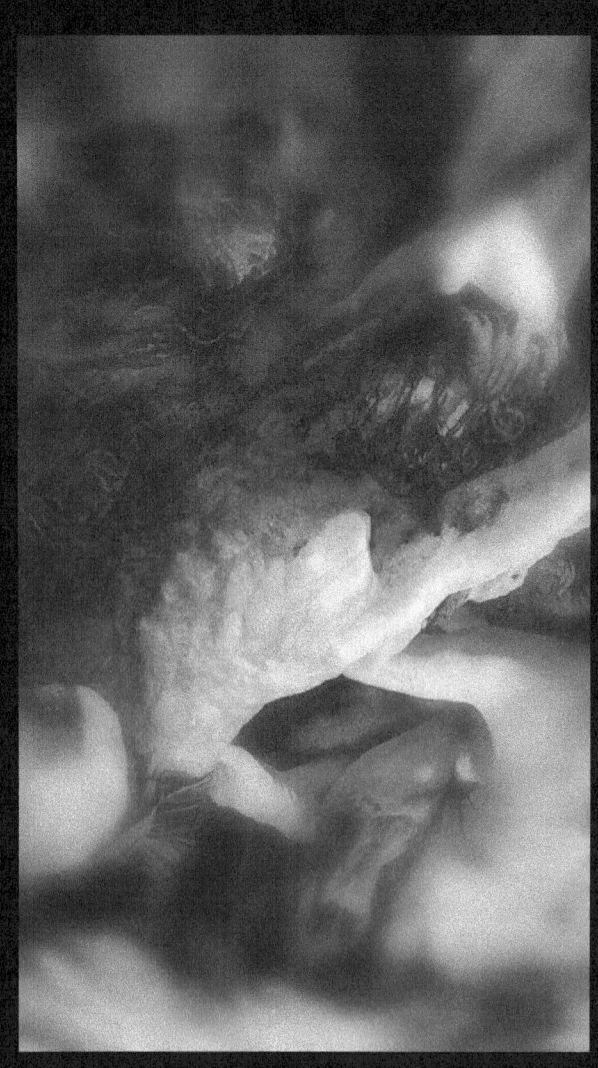

Journey of a Fallen Angel

"As if I am an inanition, a chasm, a desolation. A ruin that has started to beat and has gained a macabre pulse. I am the feeling of frozen brume settled on hiemal hands on a chill filled afternoon. I am the weep of storms. I am also as if, the black swan moribund, on an iced lake which lost its way somehow to its home; the savagery of winds. I am nature's reaping, a brier's licking of blood...
I am the crack of death in a winter's sleep."

~ Channing M, The Monochrome of Darkness

Journey of a Fallen Angel

"The marching decay on the blood-filled salver; Ascending from the table from that begrimed feed, like an aching bone, I stood on the edge of the sea – an unkind Barbarian, watching the albatross flee – for like a dizzy curse, the waters set out to be...
My eyes, that cold frozen with nonplussed death; the bleeding attire of my carcanet made... this limber dry feeling of my heart aching and fled, from seas to oceans... mingled in hell."

~Channing M, The Monochrome of Darkness

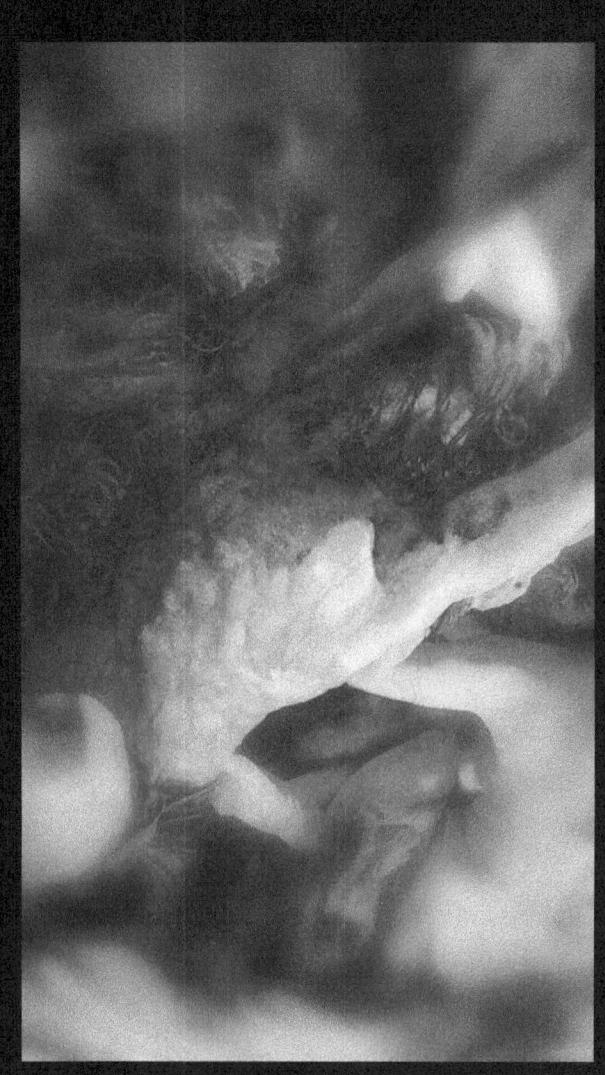

Journey of a Fallen Angel

"I am the ghost King of lost voices... living in an ocean of crystalized dust - a fort slashed with cannon fodder, blood and a lust for wicked dark whispers."

~ Channing M. The Monochrome of Darkness

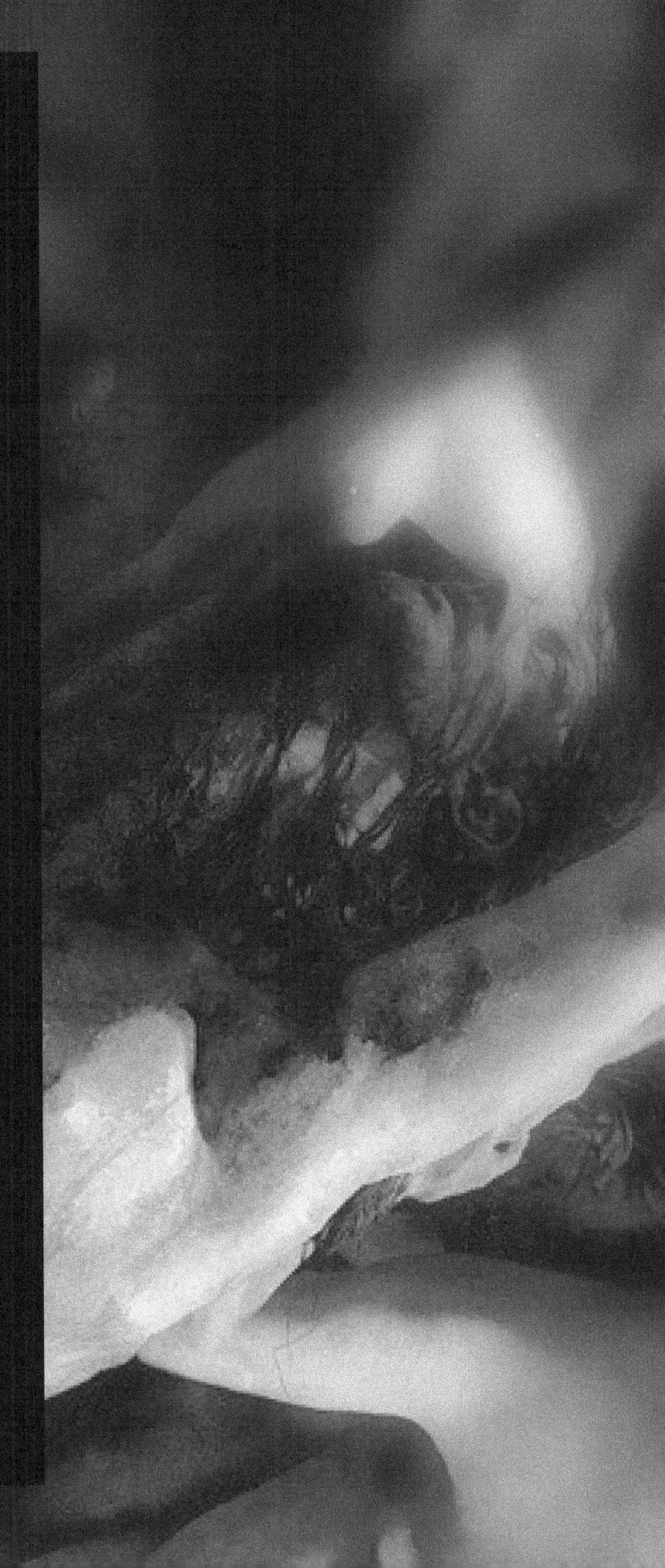

"You mourn me as though, I lay dead on a marble stone...

effaced, you look in my closed eyes, as though the storms have swept away your longings.

You are bowed at my knees like I am a healer with an ambrosial nectar.

What do you see when I am the kindness of ruthless mists?

Do you see a ghost in pain? or do you see a lover awaiting you in dead death for centuries?"

~ Channing M, The Monochrome of Darkness

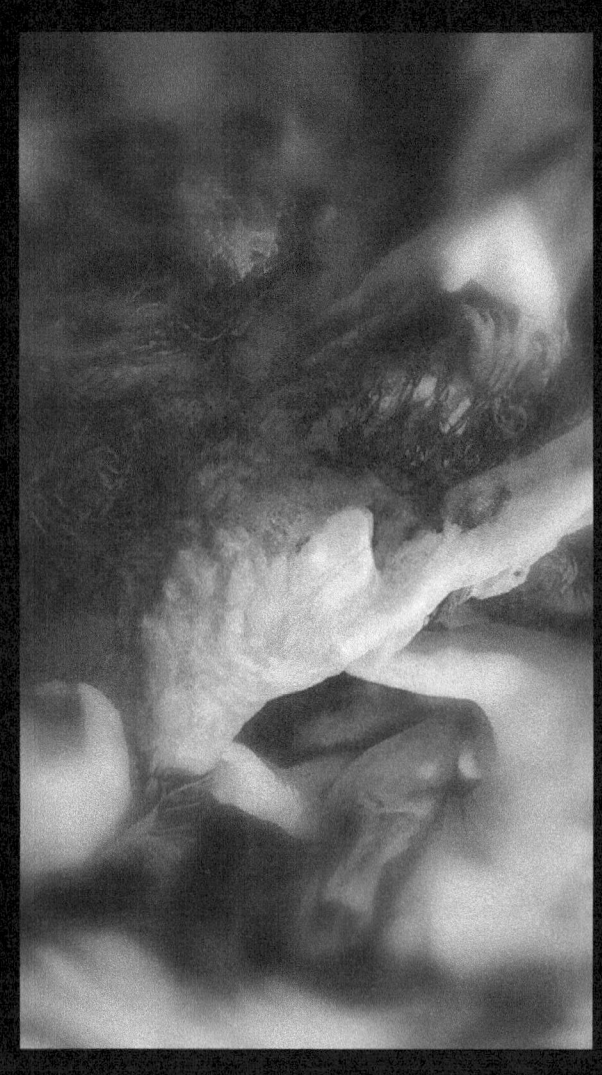

Journey of a Fallen Angel

"For I am a coffin, maimed in illness, frozen in time, in poisoned oleanders; I am the mayhem of a screeching ghost scream, whose pyre is burning inside his coffin; iced, forgotten, forlorn. I am a chained ghastly scorn of midwinter blood."

~ Channing M. The Monochrome of Darkness

Journey of a Fallen Angel

"I was the death of the moon, the chaotic crowing of an afterlife. I was a snake slithering on poisonous leaves on the days of orange night skies. I was the whisper of some doomed ghost. I was a flicking spark in the stone lying dead in cold. I was the mirror of the lakes on gloom filled evenings... I was the heart of the wild. I was wild of the heart."

~ Channing M. The Monochrome of Darkness

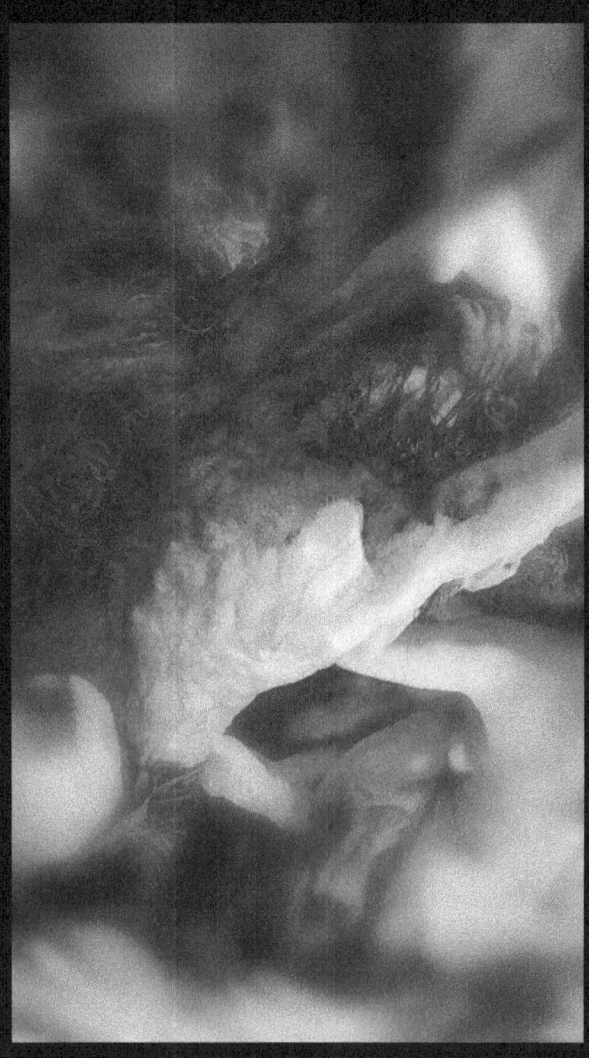

Journey of a Fallen Angel

"I love to spill blood, blood in my mind, the blood of thoughts, of regrets, of skins-

I want to murder something, brutally, savagely; I want to vulgarise my intentions, flay the tears from eyes of someone- cruelly.

I am savagery of reaping, don't tread near me, my eyes are frozen from death."

~ Channing M, The Monochrome of Darkness

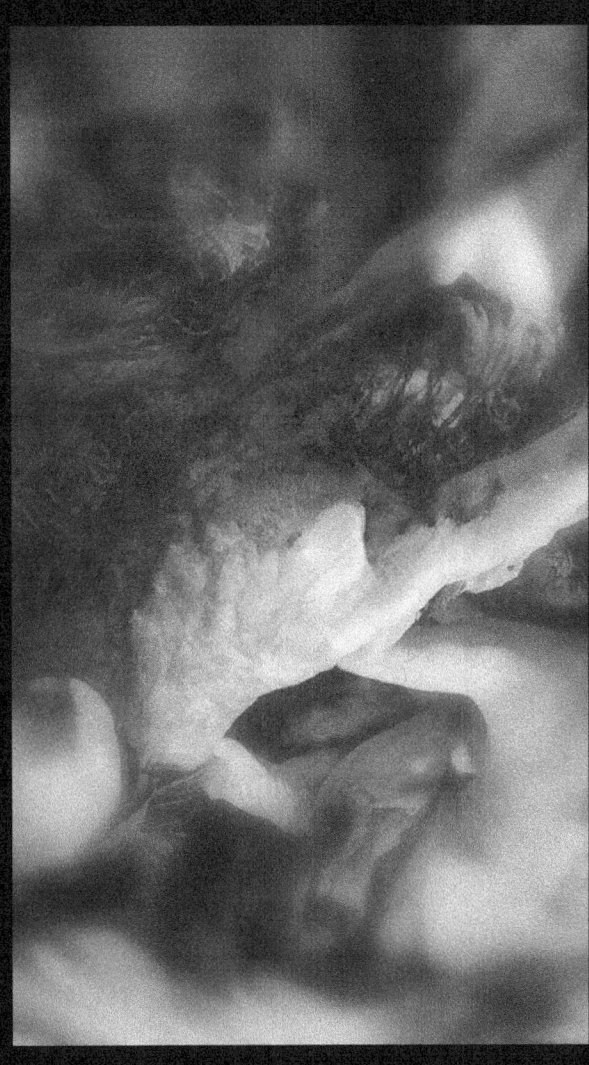

Journey of a Fallen Angel

"I am the slit in my own flesh, the barter of my own regret.

I have reaped ghosts and incised the day.

I have drowned nights and felt its' decay, for what alms do I beg for in the name of the sun?

For I am he that is doomed with a forever cursed night."

~ Channing M. The Monochrome of Darkness

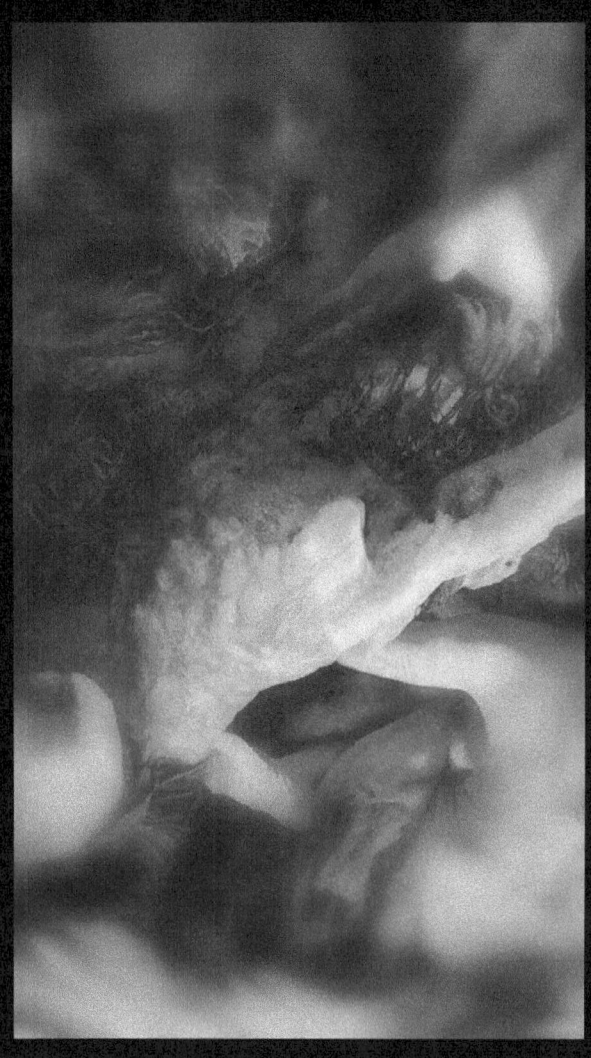

Journey of a Fallen Angel

"Bury my heart: my tired soul...

bury it down the valleys of the East, bury it where it can never be found or touched...

Bury it away from skin or flesh. Bury it away from memories, from the ardor of gazing love,

Bury it in mists, and fogs...

Bury it in the mountains of volcanic ash or the deep ocean beds, Bury it like a sour taste,

Bury it like an insanity that walks alone, Bury it immortally, Bury it."

~ Channing M, The Monochrome of Darkness

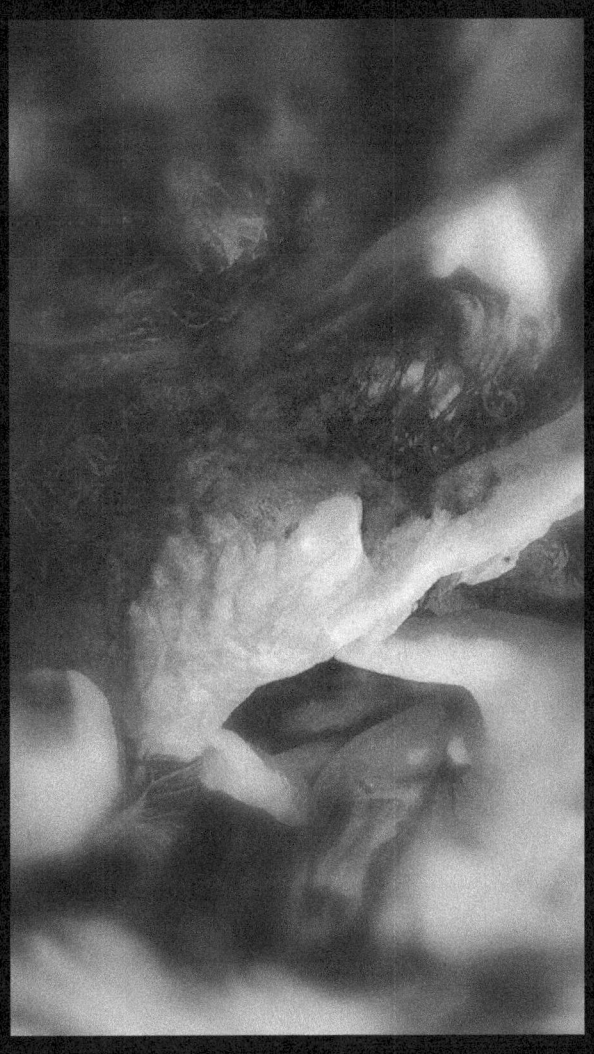

Journey of a Fallen Angel

"I was sleeping on a bed of knives, that kept cutting my flesh of sorrows. Indignant, the blade, laced with the thirst for blood, my blood; that I call a blue venom. These unbent knives, these bartered reminders of my shadow filled sighs, I am a ghost in my own bed, I am already dead."

~ Channing M, The Monochrome of Darkness

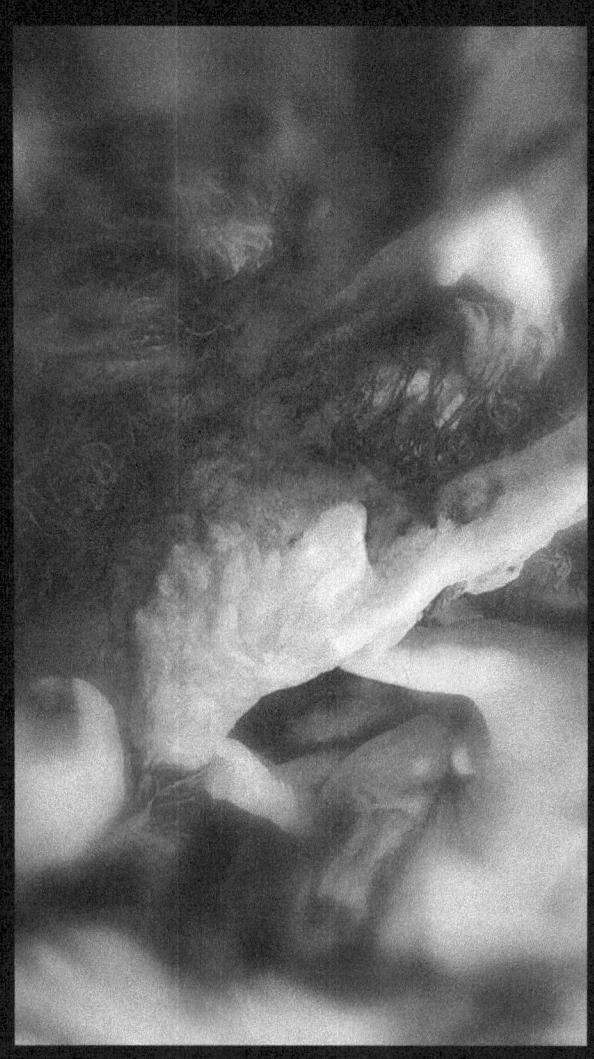

Journey of a Fallen Angel

"My skin is crippled with tears that carry no home, my footfalls, outstretches oceans, and yet cannot find a single land to build a tomb...

My eyes have frozen the blood in them, I am soulless dream of an abandoned land."

~ Channing M, The Monochrome of Darkness

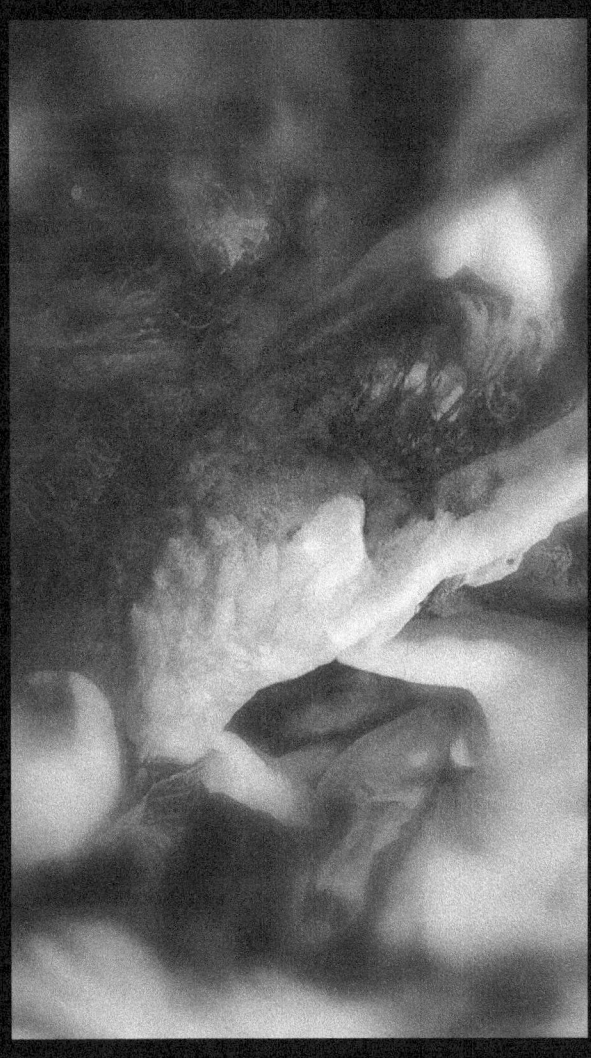

Journey of a Fallen Angel

"At times, I wish to disappear like an ancient myth, wandering in books, unaware of its touch. At times, like the withering foliage...

untouched, crumpled and gone... At times like the winds, which no one can see... At times like the heart beats, existing in bosoms yet can only be felt with pressed hands... and someday, if I do manage to become an air of senselessness, I would tap and tap like rain on the coffin of my own mortality."

~ Channing M, **The Monochrome of Darkness**

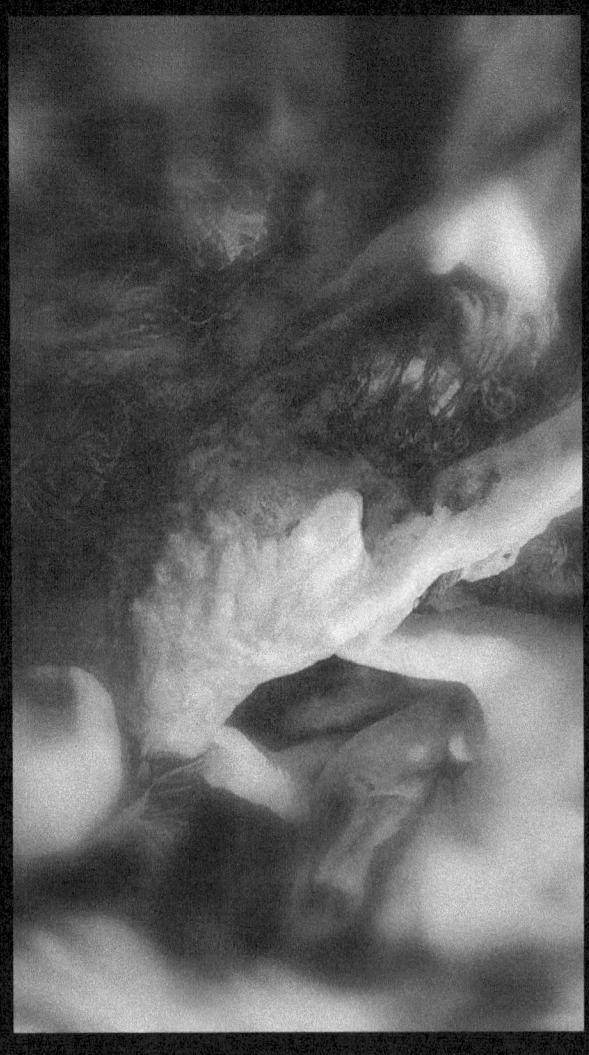

Journey of a Fallen Angel

"The cauterization on my soul, this blinding sigh, I am a sob of a jarred heart, cut me my love... cut me a cold knife, cut the heart out, I need to laugh at the Sutures I need to see me bleed. The cicatrice on the blanket of your footfalls, smile a chaos, a destruction, let's burn this house alive."

~ Channing M, The Monochrome of Darkness

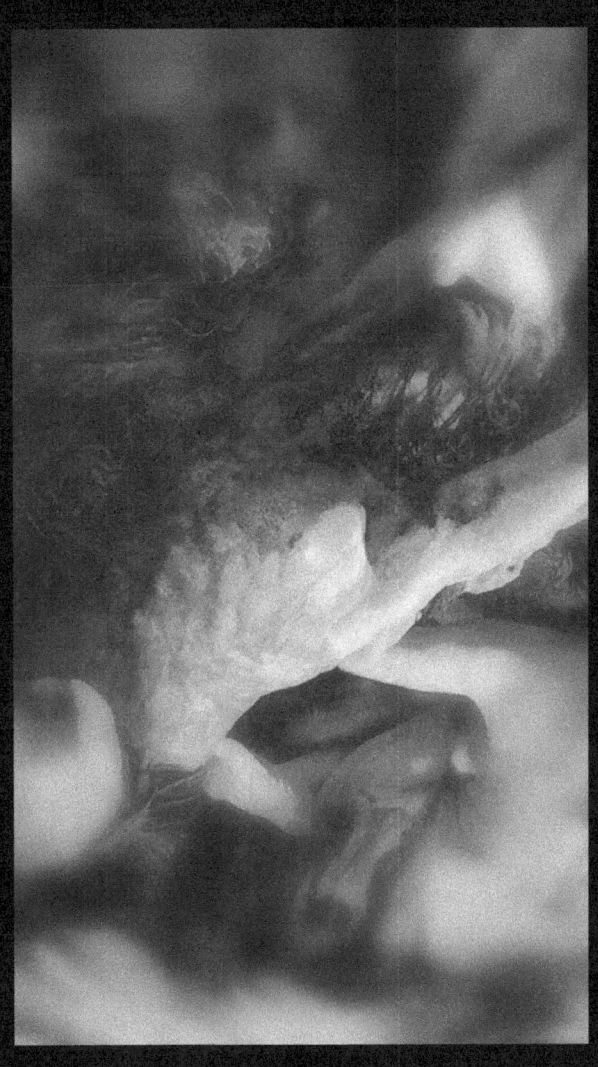

Journey of a Fallen Angel

"I am distant hurricane, a storm that has no weeping, I am the tears that carry no regrets, I am the pain, that has never forsaken a wound...

how does one idiomize a verb of desolation? Where I become the slumber for death-laden pyres."

~ Channing M. The Monochrome of Darkness

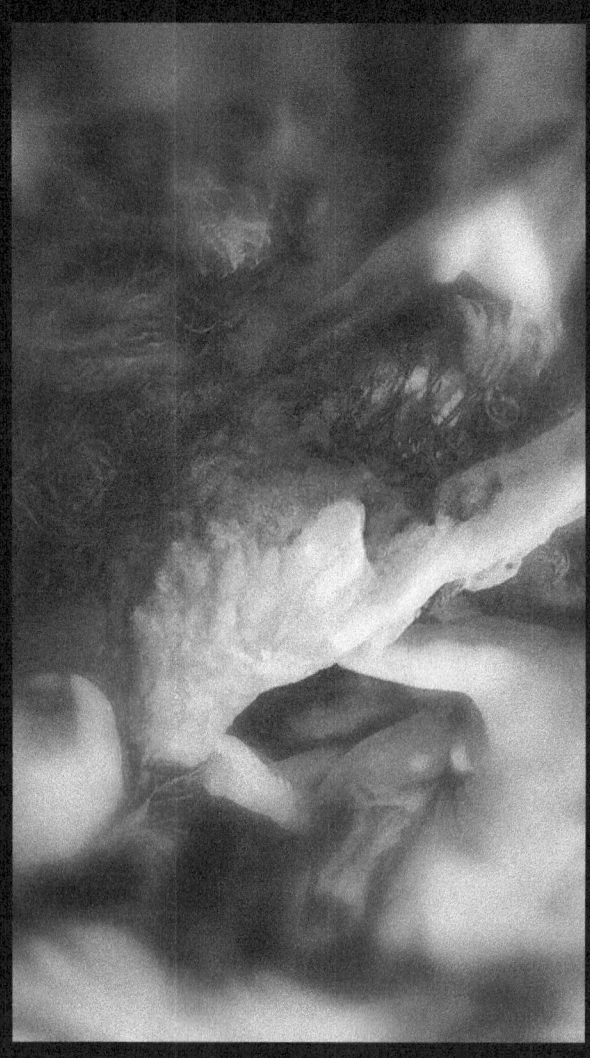

Journey of a Fallen Angel

"Like a camphor I burned, knackered in flames, knowing the extinguishing would bring respite... the insanity of these unintended breaths, this madness, her overreaching eyes, this lethargy of my infinite desires for her...

as if a hell of immortal love is afire, and only a kiss will save it."

~ Channing M, The Monochrome of Darkness

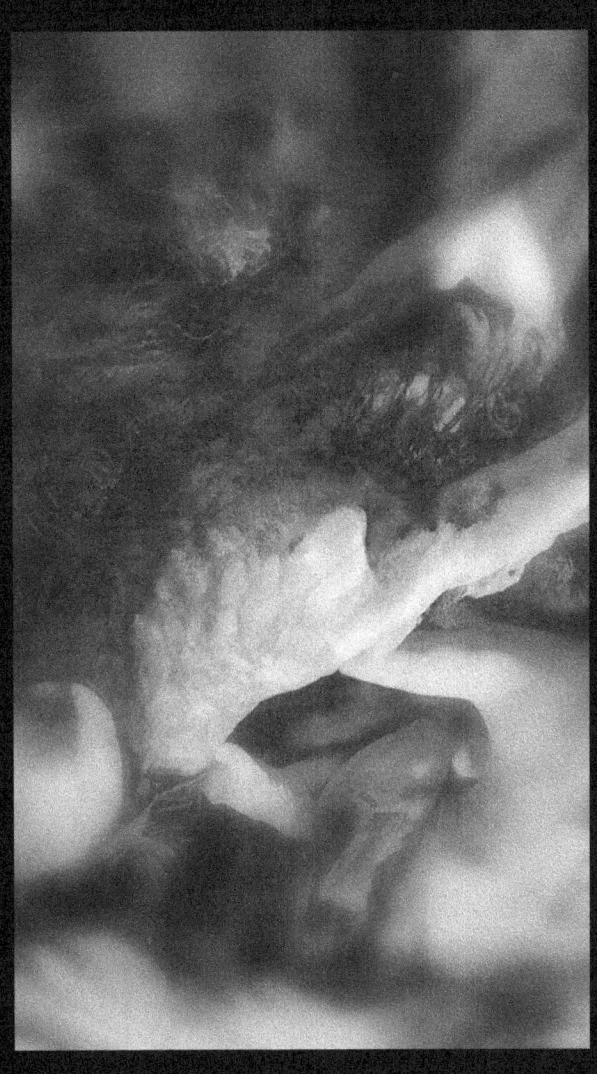

Journey of a Fallen Angel

"There was a boy, a boy I locked up in a box. I tried to push that boy into his box. It's odd to think if that day wasn't lived, would I have ever set him free? but someday... I shall open up that box again and let his disembodied spirit dance free when there is no one to see."

~ Channing M. The Monochrome of Darkness

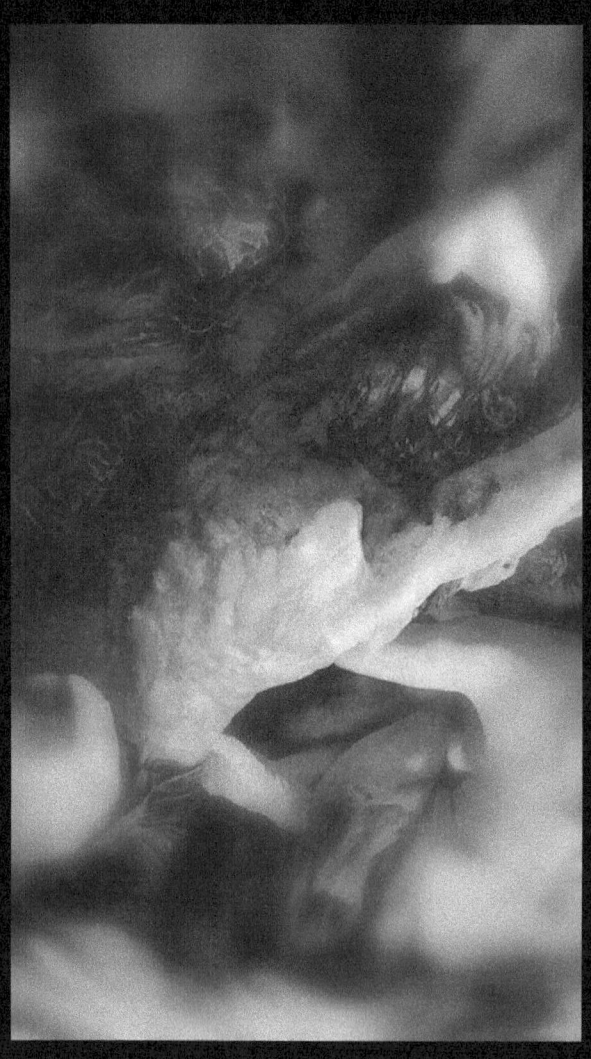

Journey of a Fallen Angel

"You are the ghastly scape of my blood driven heart, the cicatrice of my past, you are a crypt I left somewhere in the sea, you are a dark shadow, an ugly stark; I will never believe you are me."

~ Channing M, The Monochrome of Darkness

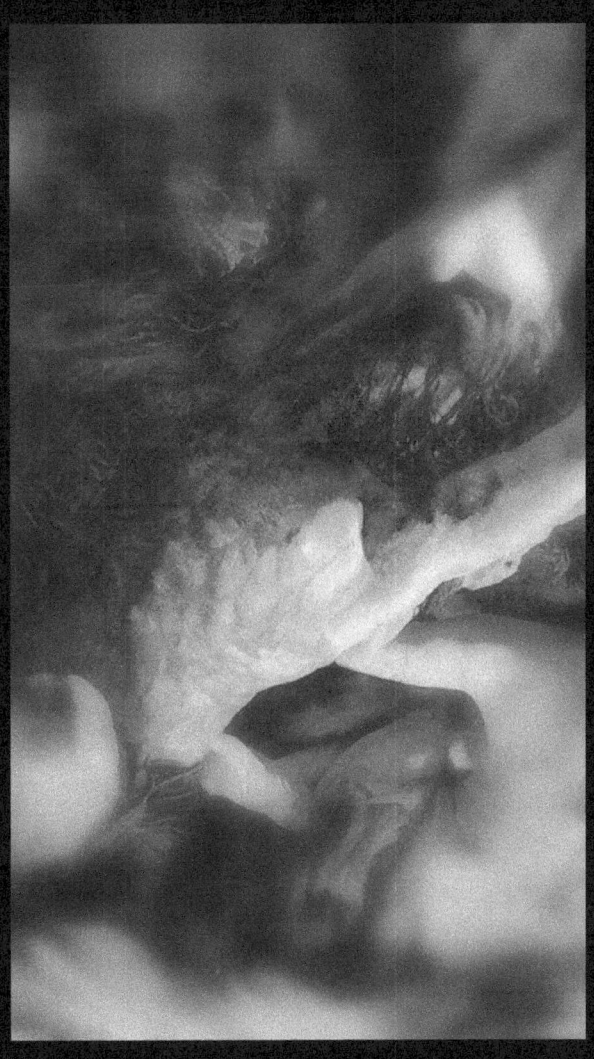

Journey of a Fallen Angel

"In darkness? or coarse beneath, his loud heart, his apparition set free, in burned thorns, his eyes, lay bare... a rose garden, an epitaph of decay. For slumbers his soul beneath ashes of wounds, toiling day and night like an aching moon."

~ Channing M. The Monochrome of Darkness

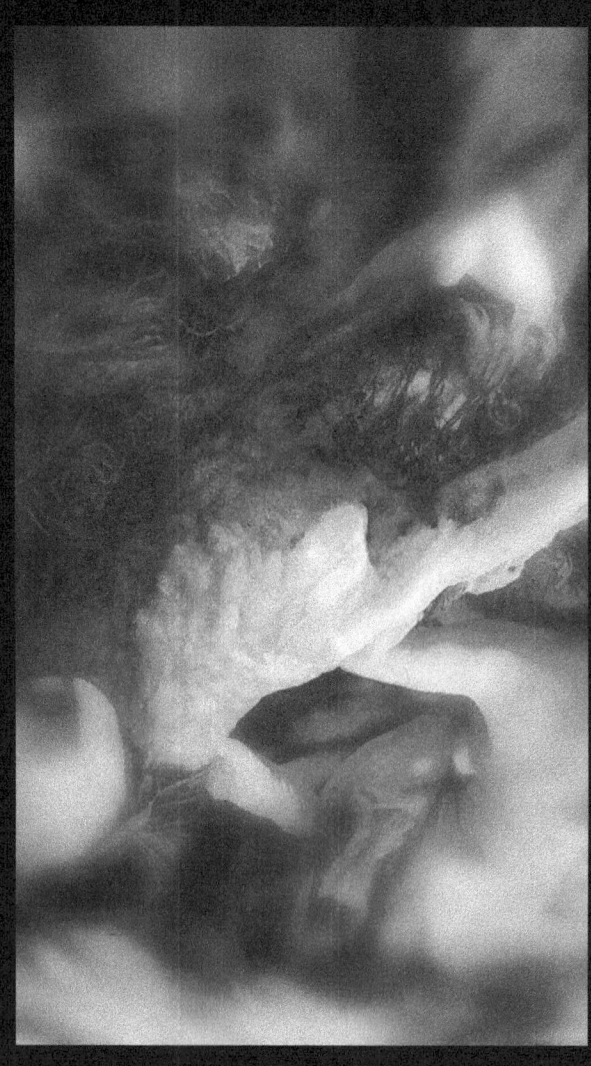

Journey of a Fallen Angel

"In the calmness of cold, dim, shadowed glass lit rooms,

the ivy-laden curvature of margent moths...
I see your shadows, walking past the stairwell of gas-lit chandelier...
My heart, that fluttering, dances around your ghostly walks...
unmoving...
bleak...
forever..."

~ Channing M, The Monochrome of Darkness

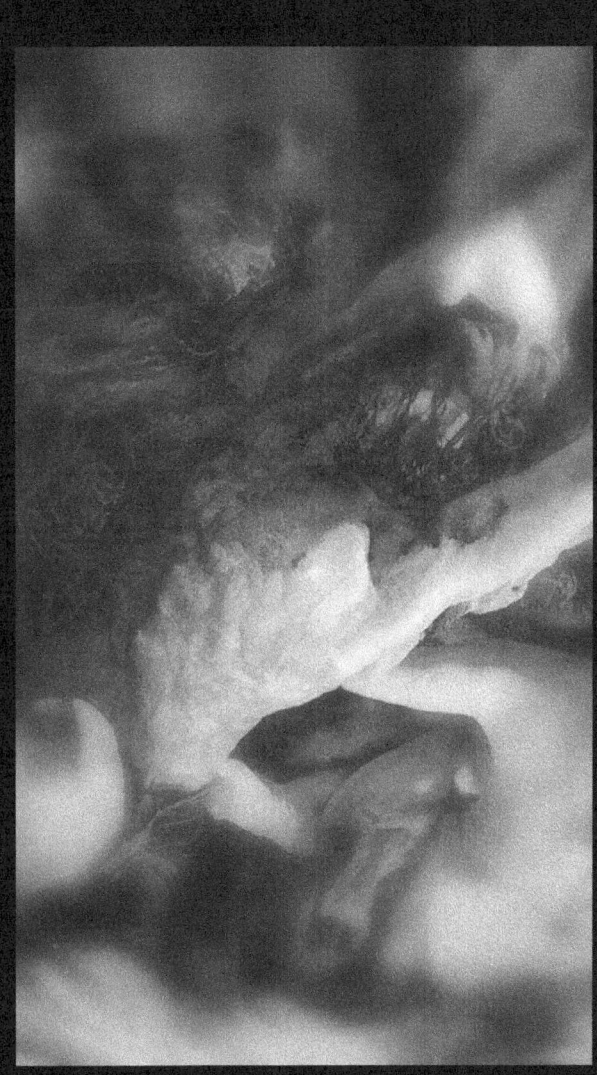

Journey of a Fallen Angel

"Tonight, this night, I feel like a Chandelier, hanging from the roof of torrential murderous skies..."

~ Channing M. The Monochrome of Darkness

Journey of a Fallen Angel

"The Canticle of my flesh, the draining, as if decaying in a thousand rotten cores, as I eat my own heart like a serpent who eats his own tail, mercilessly."

~ Channing M. The Monochrome of Darkness

Journey of a Fallen Angel

"Glancing upon the empty chariot, that of the sun Goddess, that she was, in her auroral beauty; my heart, it touched the Grecian seas and couldn't help but boast the immortal love that I harbored in my bosom for her pale gold feet, the way she had taken my heart replacing it with her immortal kiss, in which I laid, unknowing, that desires can sometimes be the fatality of Kingdoms."

~ Channing M. Her
Fragrances/The Monochrome of Darkness

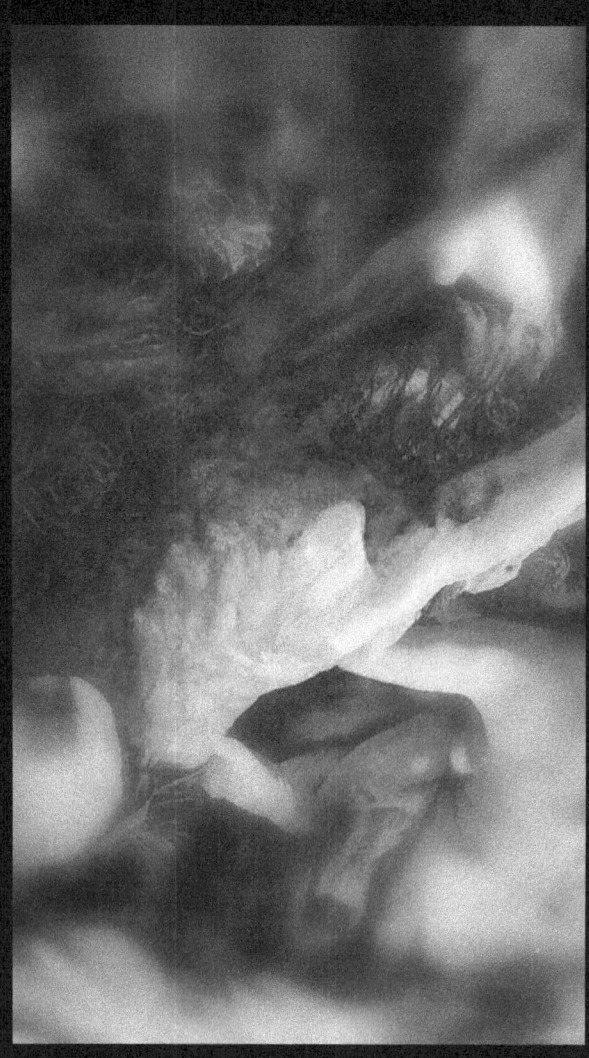

Journey of a Fallen Angel

"I am not a diaphanous beast that feasts upon the dead, nor I am the cully of foaming need, they say I am a romantic, but I am not that melody of sweet hymns, I cannibalize even in a kiss."

~ Channing M, The Monochrome of Darkness

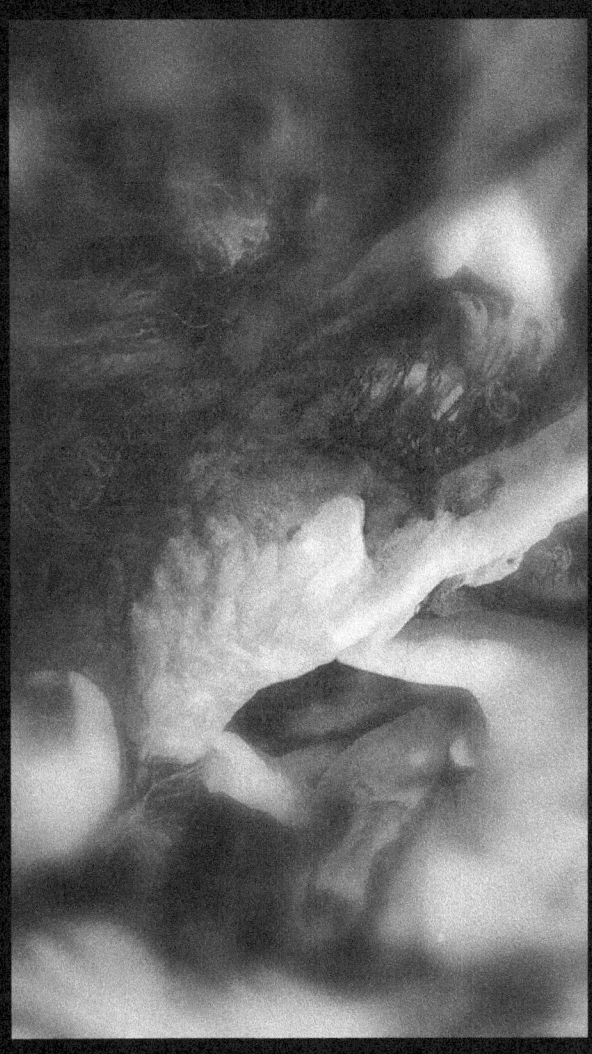

Journey of a Fallen Angel

"My stamped passions, these cold red commands, a slumber- that my pain forgets. Weeping, tearing the heart, I am the autumn's brokenness, it's withers. Your arms, your hands, touching me- will find nothing but scars and decay."

~ Channing M. The Monochrome of Darkness

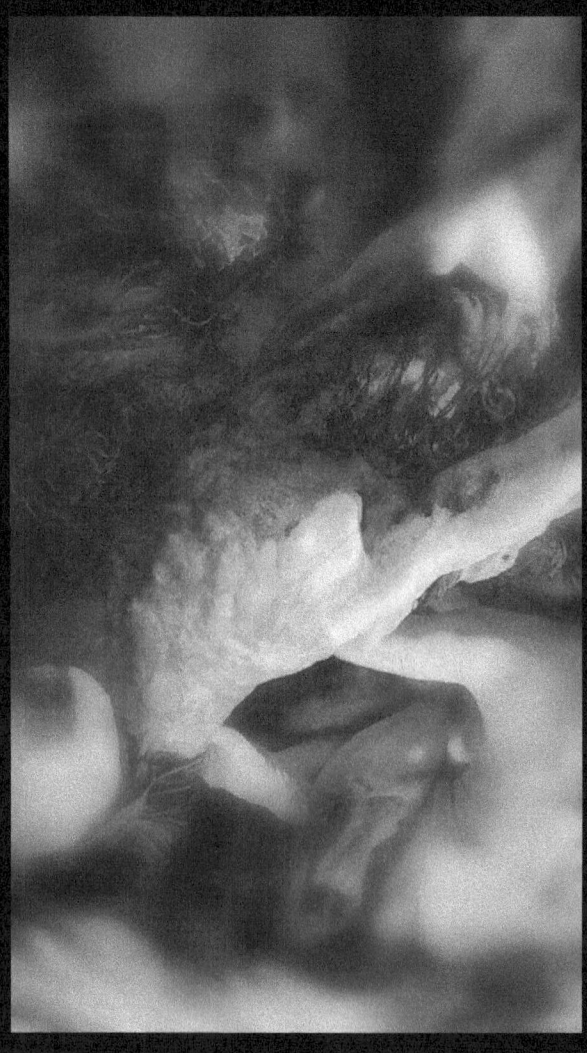

Journey of a Fallen Angel

"This mockery of a pain, this paradoxical ointment, that so far the Pastors' preach, for snakes are born nothing more of vicious poison, and under the sun I am a masquerade of deceitful imagery, and Under the moon I am the flesh of macabre portraits. Yes, you can rule my words out of eloquence... for I am nothing but a viper who eats his own tail, who bargains his own fate and who lives many deaths. My heart is concealed forever in cloaks of poison."

~ Channing M. The Monochrome of Darkness

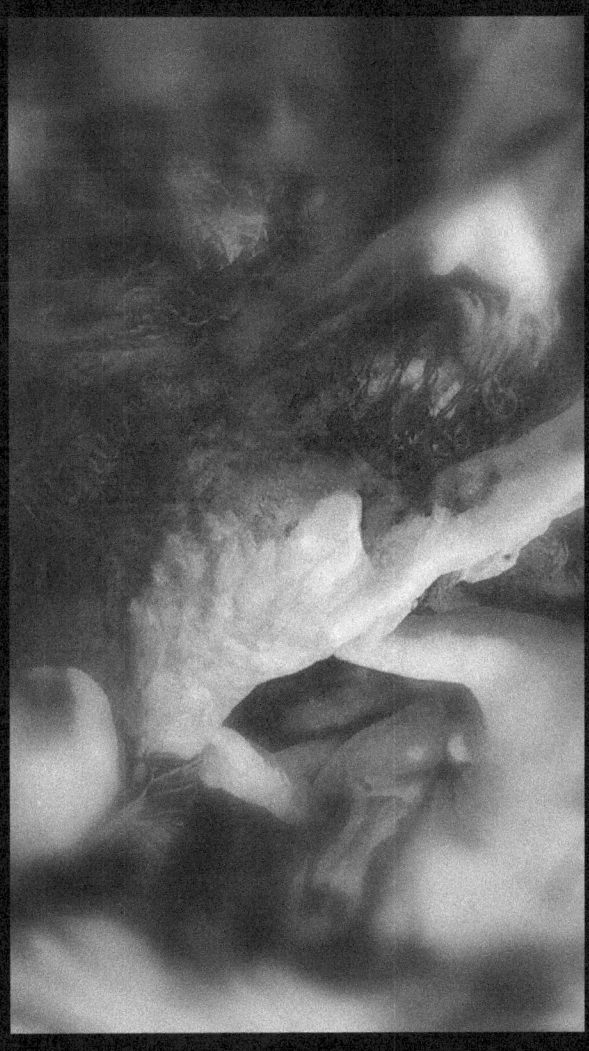

Journey of a Fallen Angel

"Those infernal eyes, draw frozen breaths in your name, as if in betrayals, in gestures, in ruination, lost in the dearth of a blazing barrenness.

why lost? I gave you all the wishes I had and these airs, they confounded me..
I am not your last sigh, your armor or your heart.
I am not your decay, your death, I am simply the start of my own end."

~ Channing M, The Monochrome of Darkness

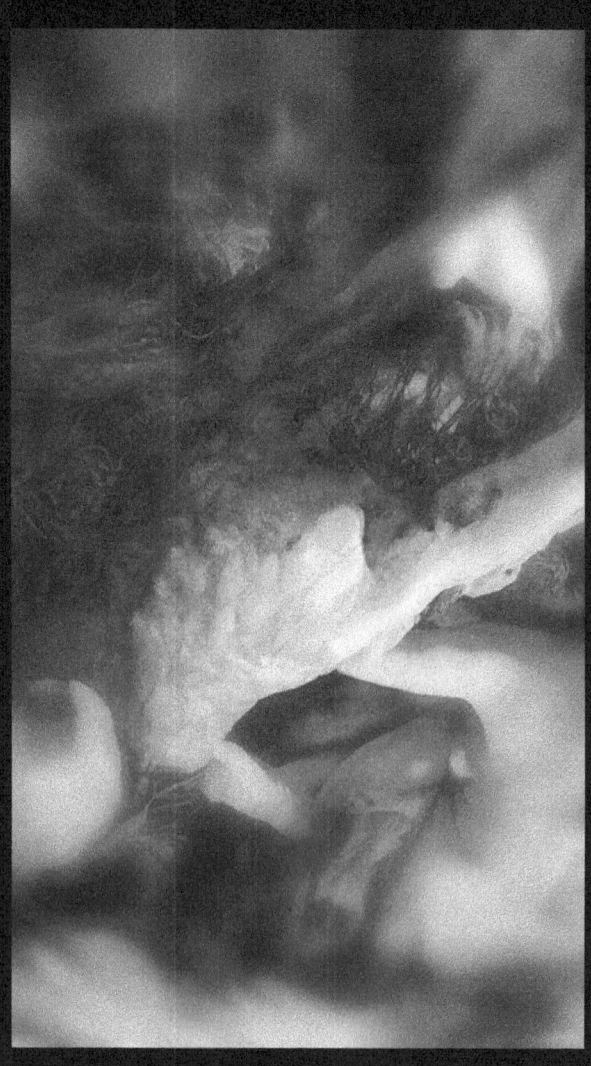

Journey of a Fallen Angel

"I burn in a viscous light of dark embers, the landscape my eyes see are full of blood and screams, as though the temple bells are ringing from somewhere far off. I am losing the dimensions of objects my eyes form, crawling to a grave of infinite abyss."

~ Channing M, The Monochrome of Darkness

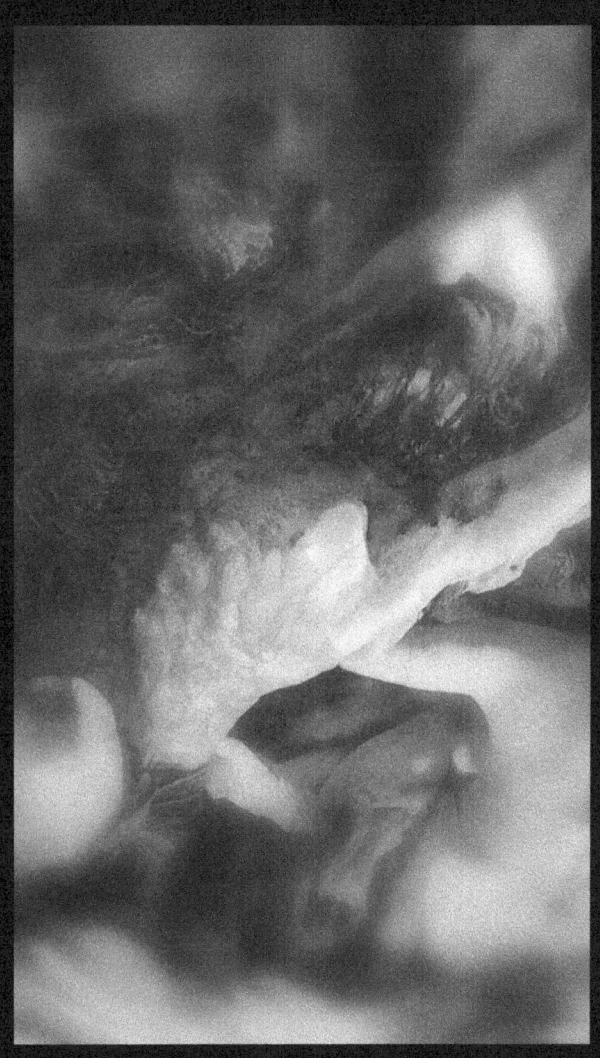

Journey of a Fallen Angel

"I am a horror that someone created and then became frightened of."

~ Channing M, The Monochrome of Darkness

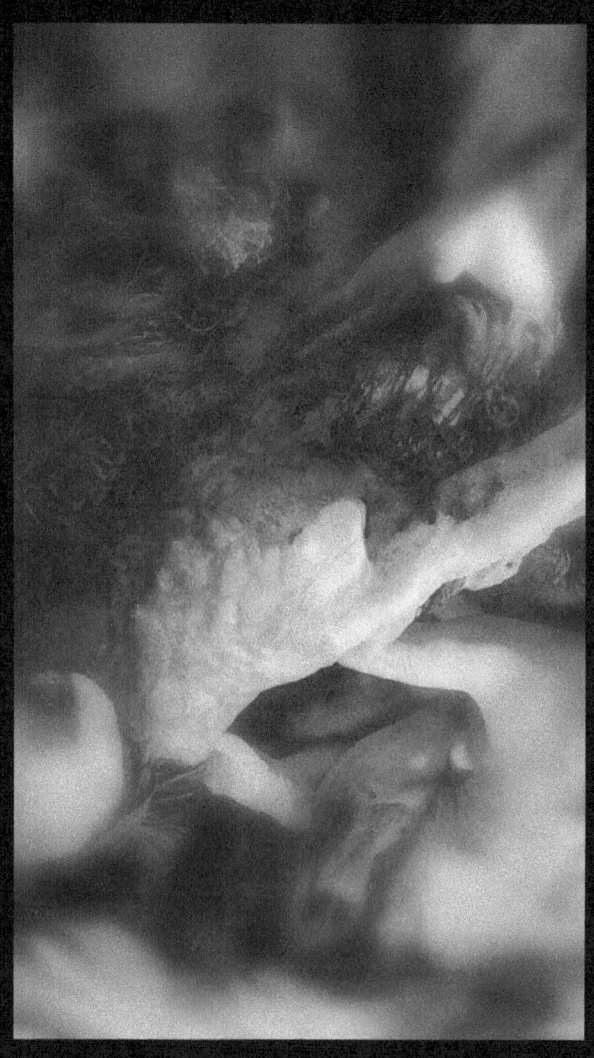

Journey of a Fallen Angel

"I am the greyness of marshland fogs', my eyes – the grey Cathedrals of abandonment, my hands as iced as a frozen pyre: Long lies the distance between the beats from my heart, the dark undertones of my footfalls, as if drawing a roadmap to the horrors of my door, this hour of fleeting breaths, the cauterization of my soul."

~ Channing M. The Monochrome of Darkness

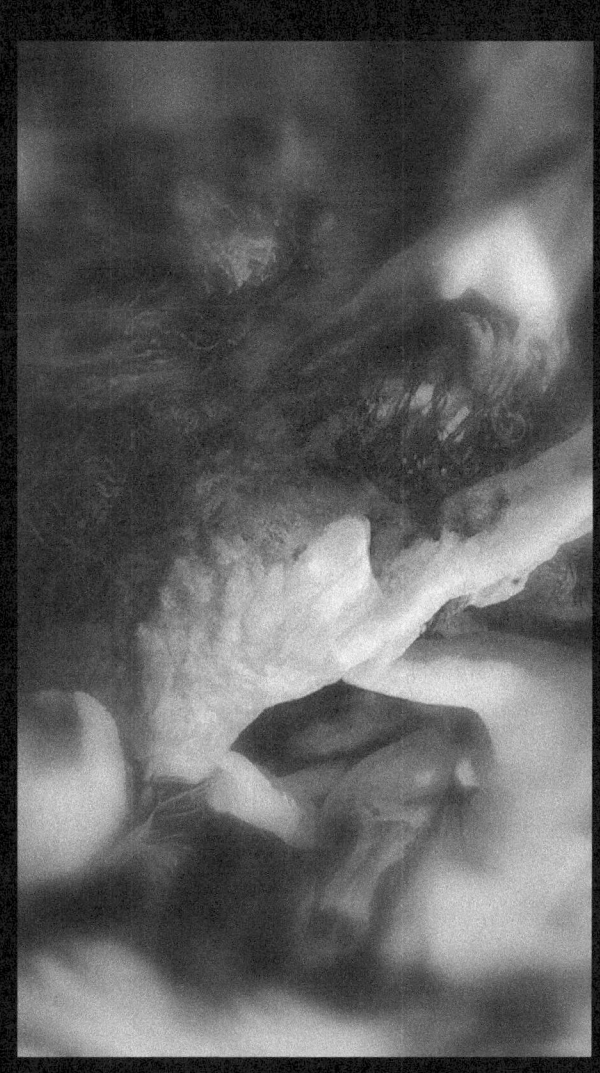

Journey of a Fallen Angel

"It's terrifyingly monstrous how one can hold such a grotesque tale inside him, shut tight and full of blood."

~ Channing M, The Monochrome of Darkness

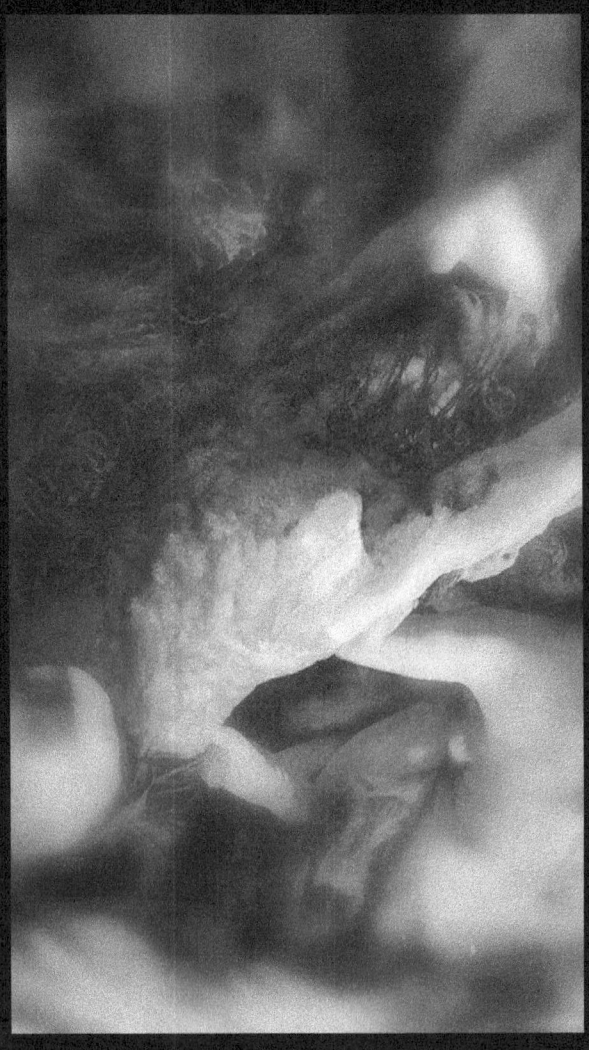

Journey of a Fallen Angel

"A parting lance, I pulled out of my heart - a forest filled with untamed wounds, screeching for a healing, as though died in a dismal. Becoming a haunt, I bled like the sun, becoming the dark, I burnt walls of death, a heart could just be a beating prey, but what to those who just don't live by it anymore."

~ Channing M. The Monochrome of Darkness

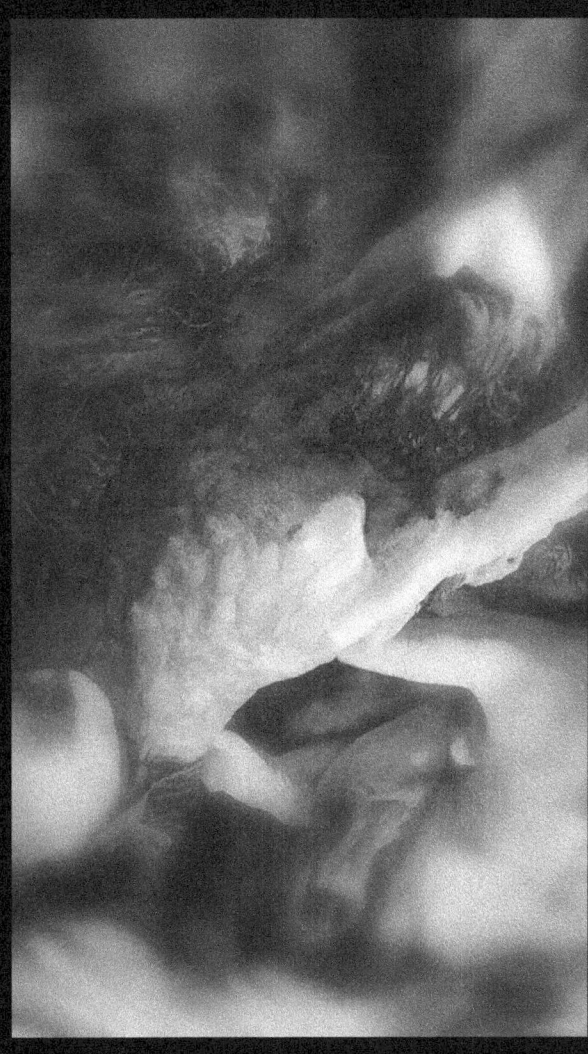

Journey of a Fallen Angel

"Quaint, my hungry heart,
Unburnish'd in the likeness of a dim sea.
Vext, forlorn like a lighthouse wandering with its shadows. Dark, gone, in its hours.
Alone, enraged, and killing."

~ Channing M, The Monochrome of Darkness

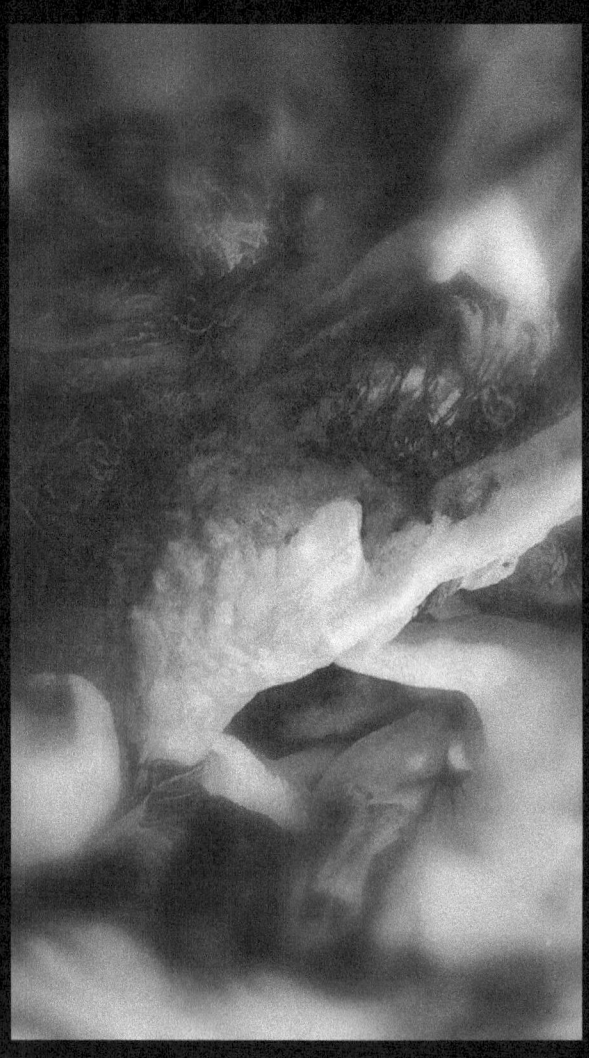

Journey of a Fallen Angel

"I have been in the dark, treading waters, gripping a red-lit paraffin lamp, the waters have turned reddish blood as if crimson has died in the arms of tormented shadows."

~ Channing M., *The Monochrome of Darkness*

Journey of a Fallen Angel

And I kept a poet's secret soul, in night's quiv'ring arms... In his garbs of fire, I lit a fatal day.

His voice, as if a fire of thousand hells, his mourn- a dirge.

~ Channing M, The Monochrome of Darkness

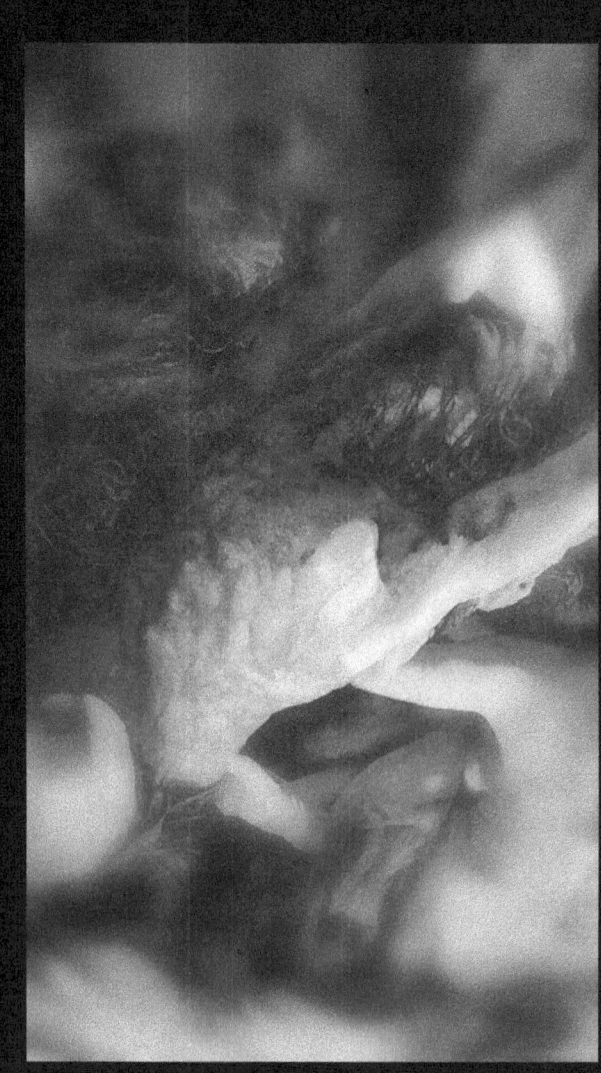

"On a dust-filled table lit on candelabras, I serve my heart on the blood-filled platter."

~ Channing M, The Monochrome of Darkness

Journey of a Fallen Angel

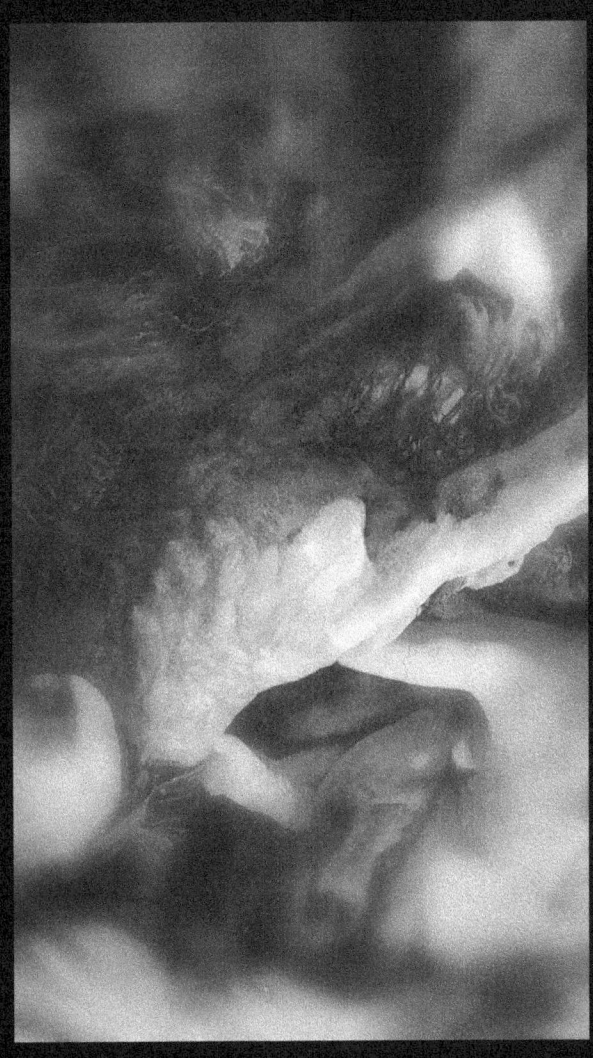

Journey of a Fallen Angel

"The smoke, it was filling his lungs with venom, and he designed a castle from it, his demented scapes of wanderings, his thirst full of empty longings and the curtains, veiled with variegated masks, flowing the chancer, as if harked with unnameable darkness, his mind, he could not un-garb, as if there was nothing behind but a wisp of smoke that filled his lungs."

~ Channing M, The Monochrome of Darkness

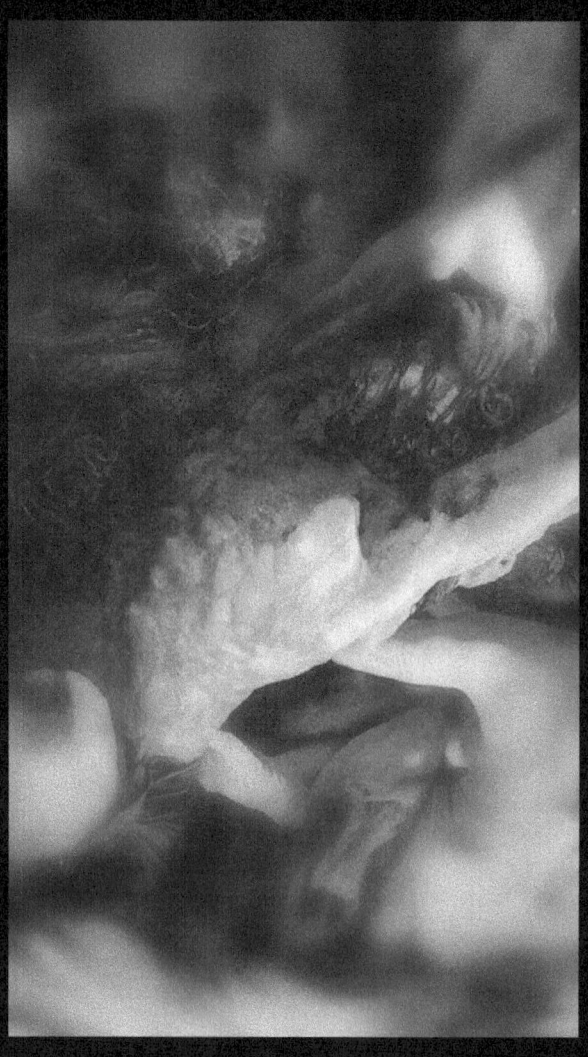

Journey of a Fallen Angel

"In the heart of an eclipse, the writer dips, his quill made of blood and wounds, sinking far in storms, he sleeps no more...

a ruin throng'd, filled in absolute despair of his wasteland of eyes...that arrests the falling sun inside a heartless venom."

~ Channing M, The Monochrome of Darkness

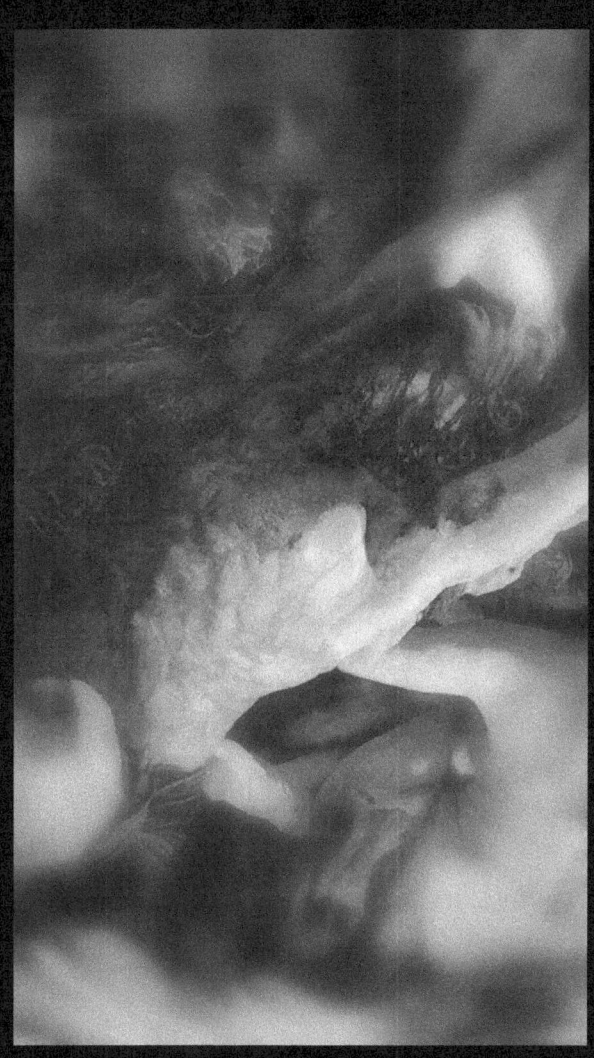

Journey of a Fallen Angel

"The tragedies that embark on with an 'invocation' of a 'muse' in the highest elation, are quite harrowing in its hamartia as if in a corollary, prayers to 'muse' always end up in a catastrophe. In simpler other words, the very formation of such a ghastly, macabre invention of a deity is the very cause of destruction."

~ Channing M,

The Monochrome of Darkness

'Hang the Muses'

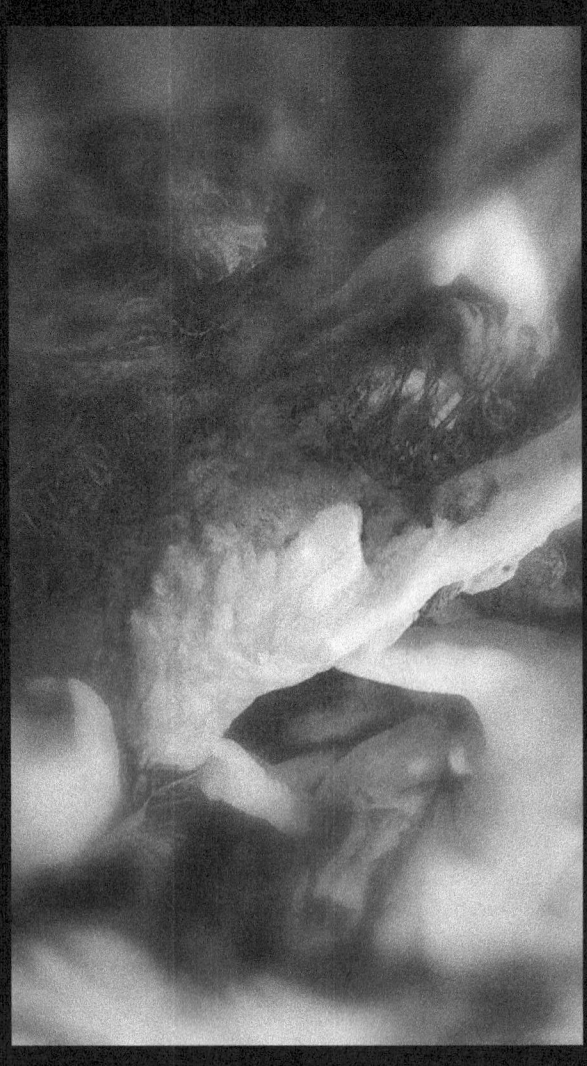

Journey of a Fallen Angel

"Of so much, clustering, a slender waste, as if he was a demon carved touching the curvature of a perfect witness, a snake...

A journey to the path of infernal waters, he sees himself, abus'd and disabus'd... not knowing whether to call himself a beast or a demonic God. His rural ancestors, his sole judge. His conscience, a rustic vein, His dark cloaks, his soul to blot."

~ Channing M, The Monochrome of Darkness

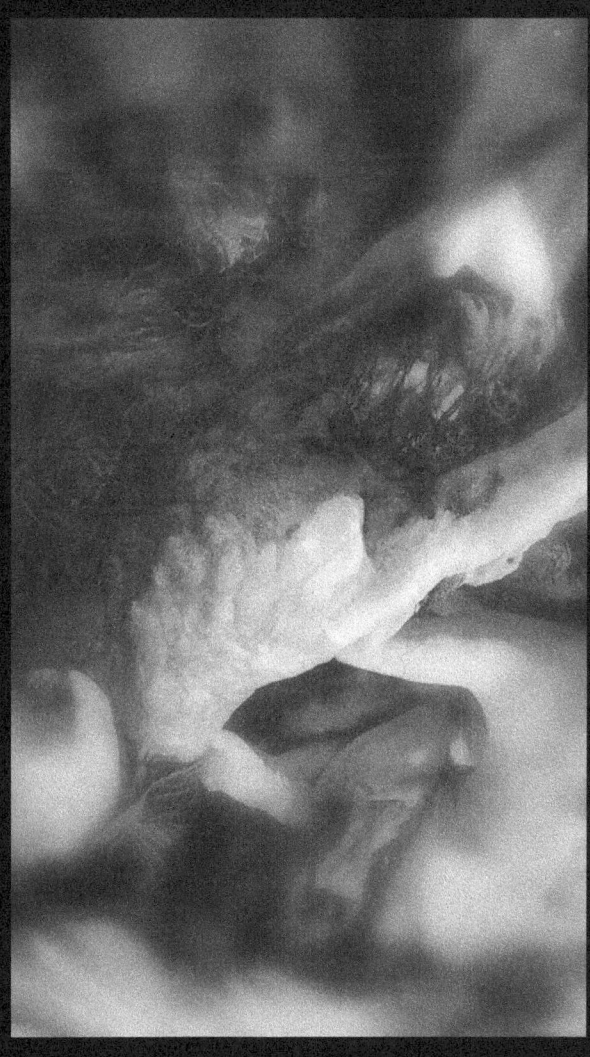

Journey of a Fallen Angel

"Unbidden arrows, my heart, it perceiv'd a pale white dawn,

in dim lights of love-laden blood-fill'd bed,

as if a grave of a hymeneal chorus, these shadows of languid hours, tired in blood and wine...

true and deep, I fall asleep in the arms of demonic nightmares"

~ Channing M, The Monochrome of Darkness.

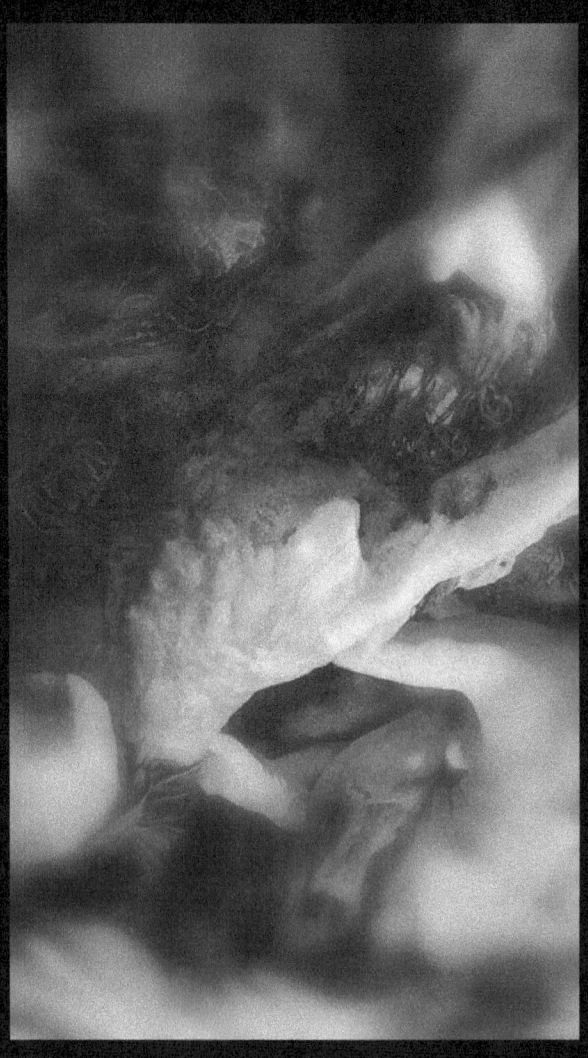

Journey of a Fallen Angel

"The travelling fawns, scaring the limbs of berried ivy, cascading venom,

hounding winter around the wolf that follows, his trails of blood for the vine,

in visible silence, a rose drips of blood."

~ Channing M, The Monochrome of Darkness.

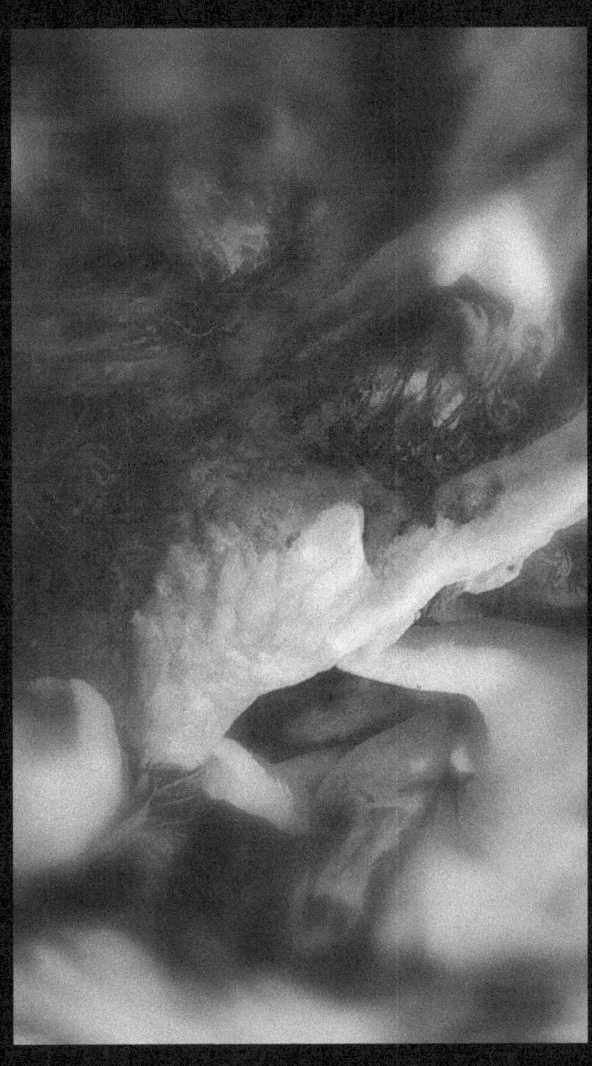

Journey of a Fallen Angel

"His heart a descant join, the ghosts that breathed and humm'd.

The scarlet letters, dripping aches of his bane...
Like six crimson devils, his eyes, a web of war;
What Carnage as if to blot the sun, his soul his... falchion.
the night's distant bloodshed, his mind- clamours.
He was the strains of immortality."

~ Channing M. The Monochrome of Darkness

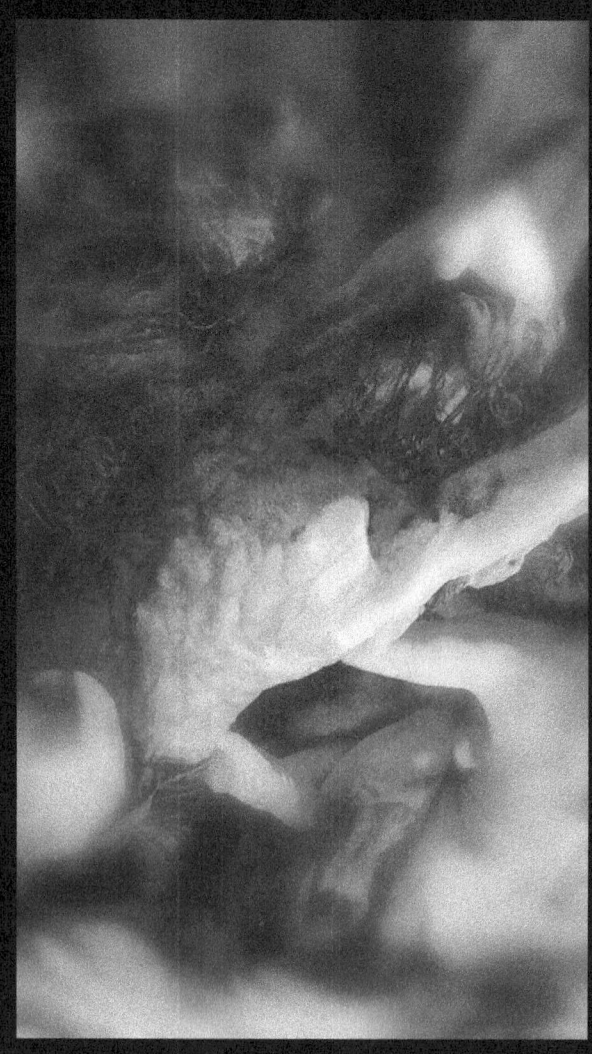

Journey of a Fallen Angel

"That day, I burned three pyres, of three ghosts, so wear the crowns that my head wore, bleeding in thorns, walk with the lance that carried my wounds, wear the cloaks of my shame, choke on my deathlike screams, you'll get weak, tremble, before you could dance even half a measure I could, I am an army of thousand ghosts whispering fire on your doom."

~Channing M, The Monochrome of Darkness

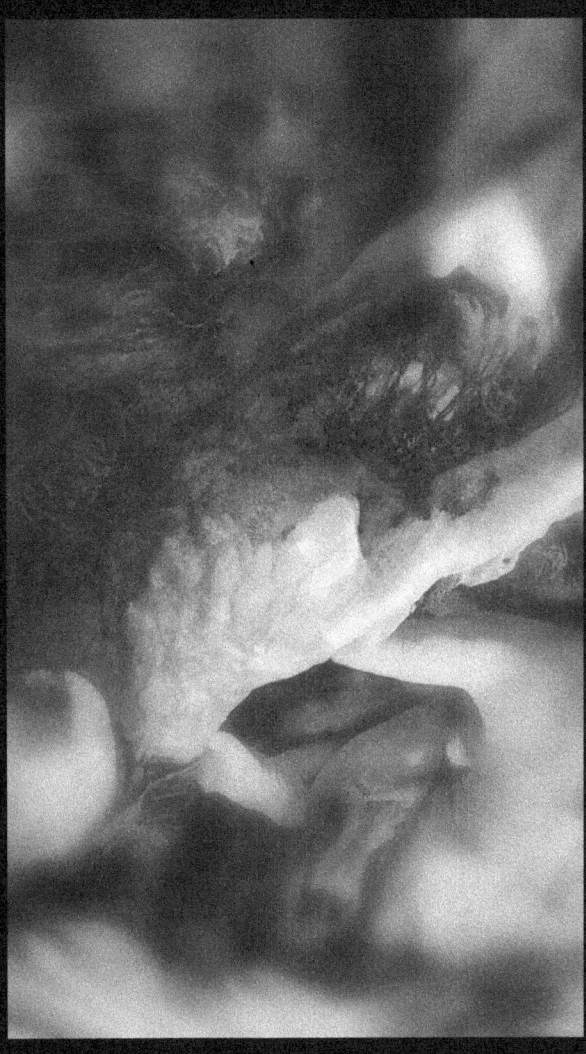

Journey of a Fallen Angel

"Condemn'd alike his madness, to groan,

For the solemn stillness in his pale skin holds
The night shades her own skin with the darkest mold,
The hooting owl perches on the lamenting copse, to Molest night's antiquat'd solitary reign
He whispers cold breaths in the ear of dauntless Death."

~Channing M. The Monochrome of Darkness

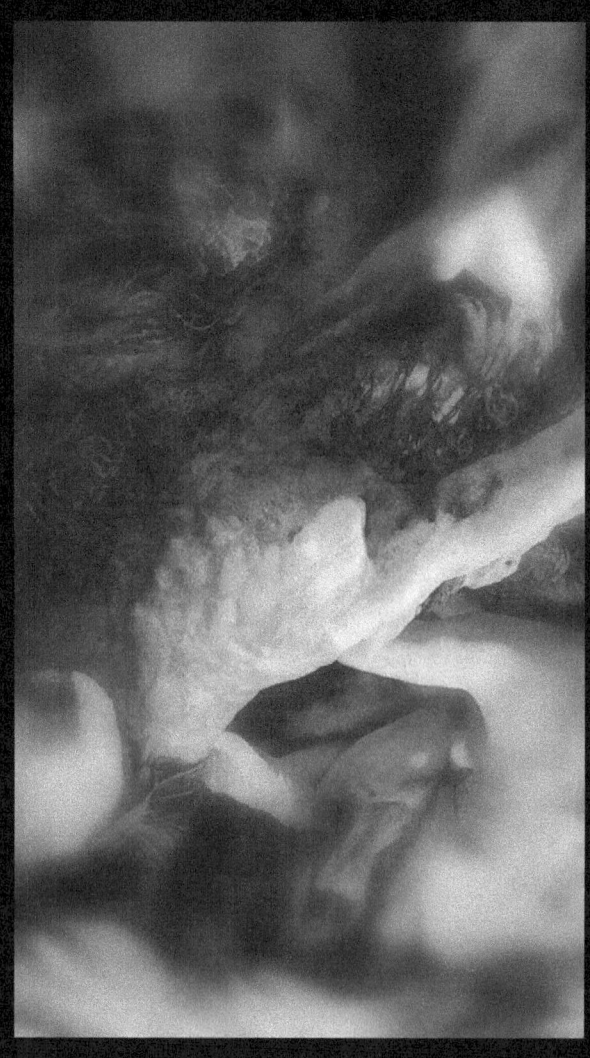

Journey of a Fallen Angel

"Some memories, I just wish I could burn them aground, shut doors, as if grief could be locked away and its key found at oceans' deepest floor. If I could erase, my heart would not exist, it has eviscerated itself, hurt on scars, but I am a dreamer and a lover, and sometimes, just sometimes, some things are written on the palette of forever."

~ Channing M. The Monochrome of Darkness

Journey of a Fallen Angel

"I am the unknown whispers of the dark hallways I tread. The darkness, how it disintegrates into a deeper one, leaving the world shallower. How many ghosts breathe inside my skin, how pale my veins beat, I have no idea if I can taste mornings anymore, as if I have been walking in an everlasting night."

~Channing M, The Monochrome of Darkness

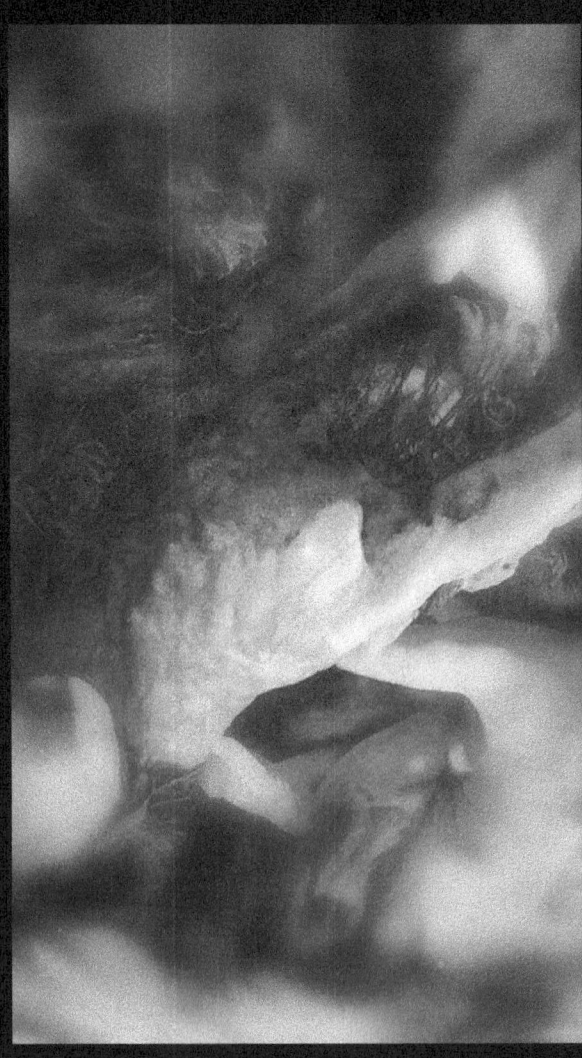

Journey of a Fallen Angel

"The early morning smells of frankincense lingered across the corridors of the Chapel. He stood there anointed in the smell, the breeze carried to him, always so full of melancholic hues, his footfalls - in ways he moved his lips to form words, he could make anyone follow him even inside a burning church"

~ Channing M, The Monochrome of Darkness

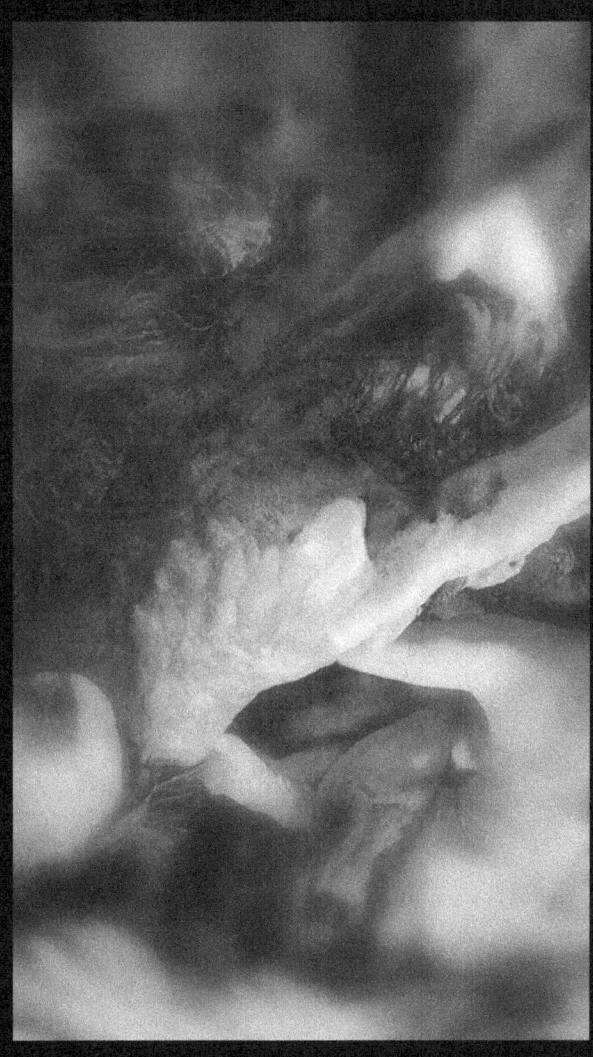

Journey of a Fallen Angel

"murm'ring margent hours,
in languish I have decay'd
in reigns of glassy waves or heart's terrain
a tear shed, was I a wound of doom?"

~Channing M, The Monochrome of Darkness

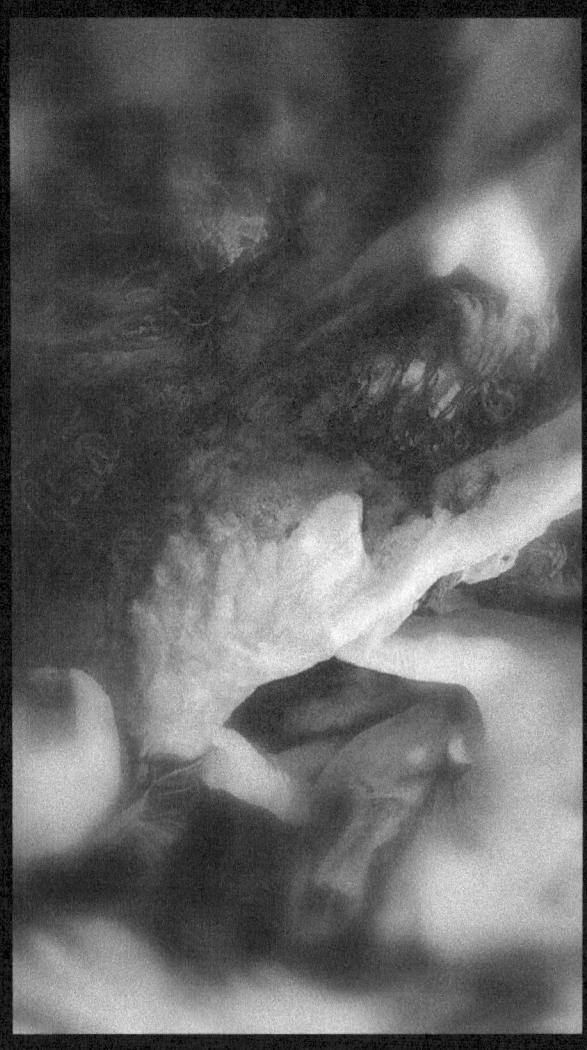

Journey of a Fallen Angel

"In the name of madness, I made him a poet.

Who walked his weary ways on the bridges of Arcadian scapes, his wounds, efflorescent canvases scudding along the couloir of Florence halls. I never made him of this world. Rather of worlds lost in eras. I made his bed amidst the creaks of Victorian London; I made his calamus for penning culled in gardens from Elysium. For me, he was never a mortal flesh. Rather, the cruelest horror one can invent in the name of mad blue drops of ink."

~Channing M. The Monochrome of Darkness

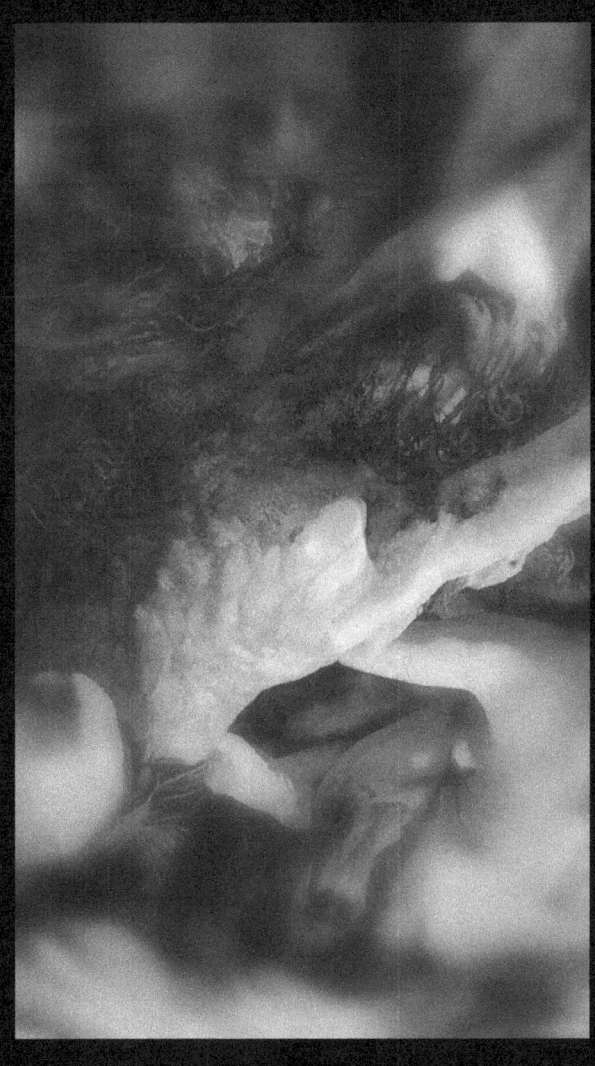

Journey of a Fallen Angel

"I am the language of sin, undeterred, the cross on my chest is turned upside down, I am the blasphemy of holy wars, thorn'd, ivy-laden is now the moth-eaten heart that has become cobwebbed in eras, am I the claw of your thoughts or am I your bleeding tears, is there a word for winds that fall on the ground before it's demise?"

~Channing M, The Monochrome of Darkness

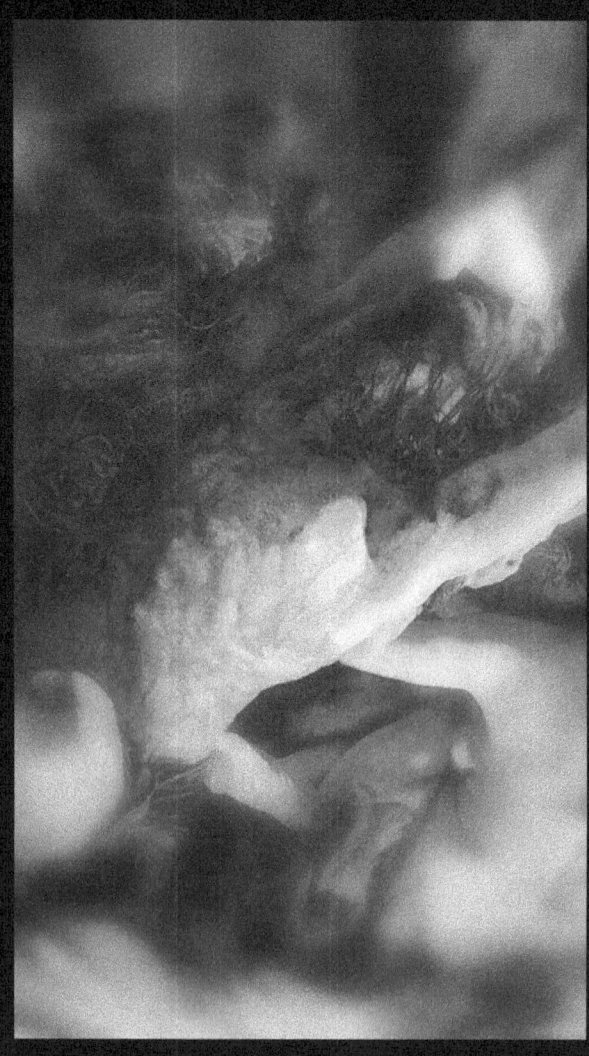

Journey of a Fallen Angel

"His eyes were like armorial armories, they had seen savagery for wounds, ruins made of heartlessness, graves made of rotting hearts, the cold had frozen to death in his eyes."

~Channing M. The Monochrome of Darkness

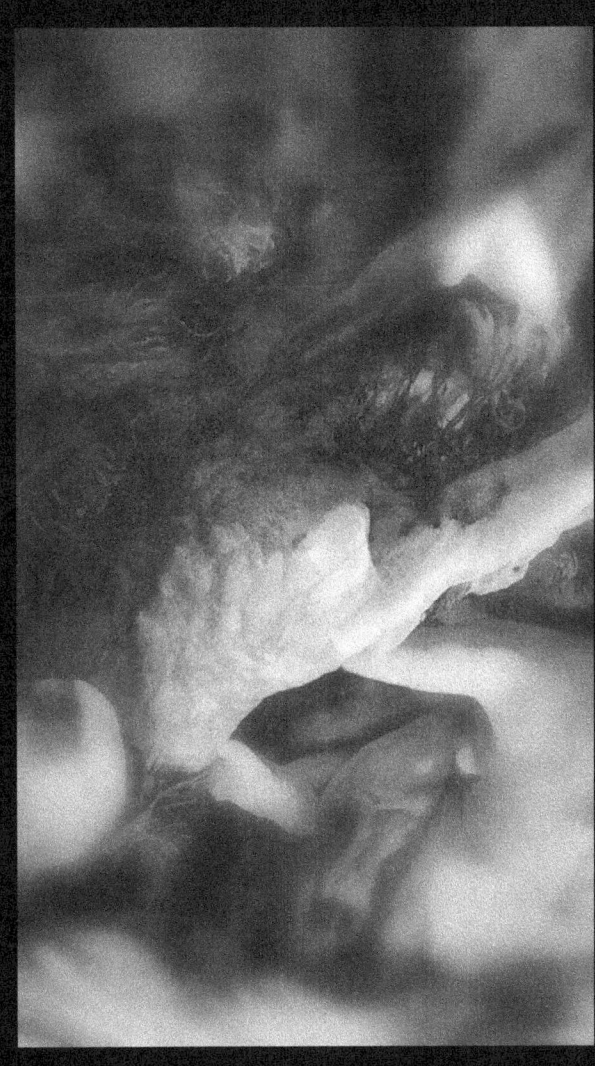

Journey of a Fallen Angel

"Look, O Heav'ns, Your betrayals, Your carnage upon me and rot."

~Channing M, The Monochrome of Darkness

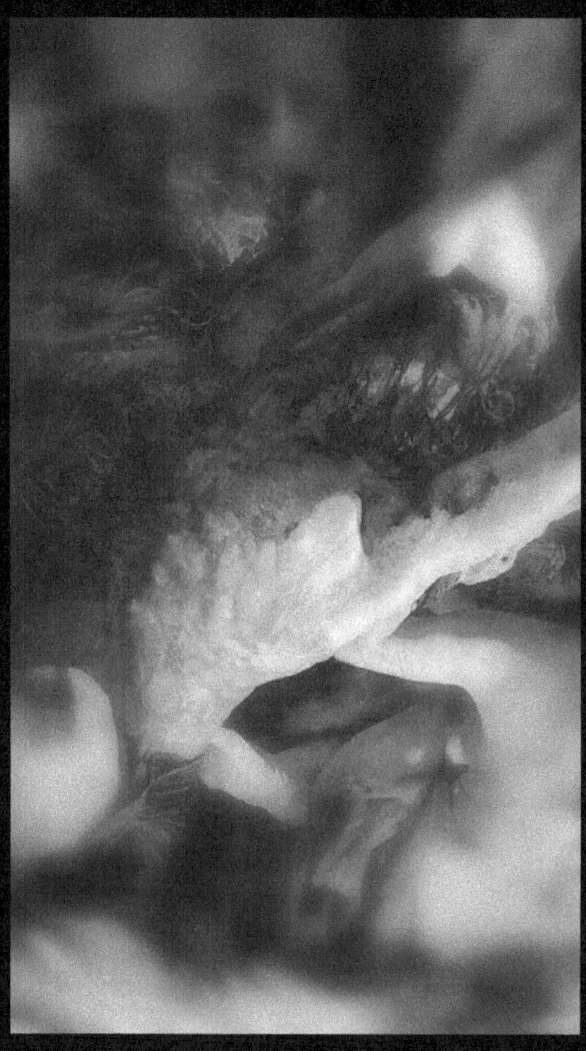

Journey of a Fallen Angel

"Visag'd decaying in his despair
beneath the wings of alter'd mortal eye
His veins, his vitals rage commence."

~Channing M. The Monochrome of Darkness

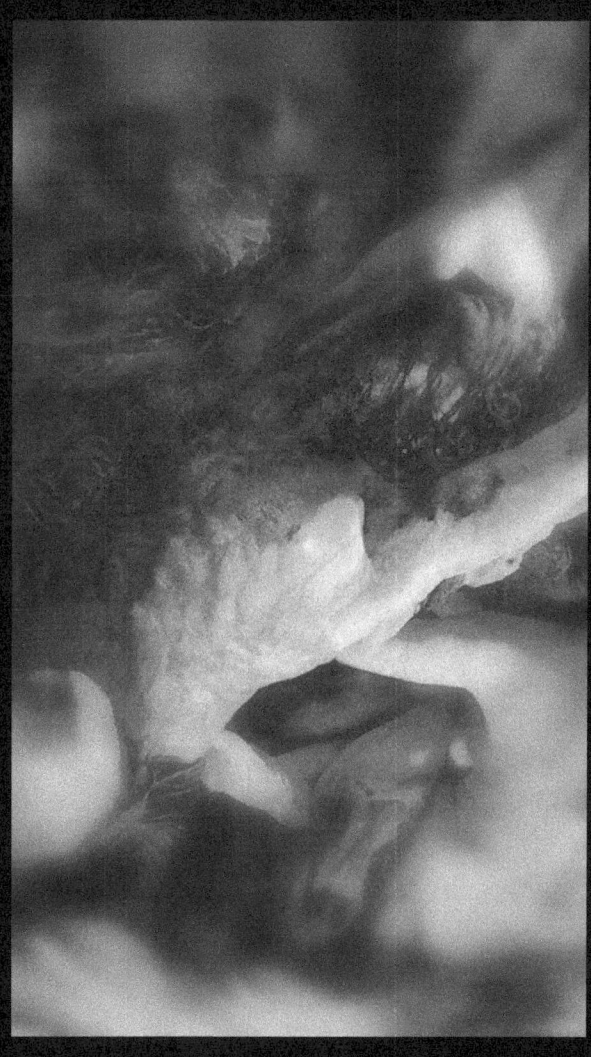

Journey of a Fallen Angel

"A hoard of dark ships journeyed till the end of my soul, and by and by, the winds lost its barbarity, wavering, desultory it began to fade away from the sharpness that once salient, now foregone. To my shaded heart, I search research for those winds that now fade away at the egress, frozen in congruence."

~ Channing M. The Monochrome of Darkness

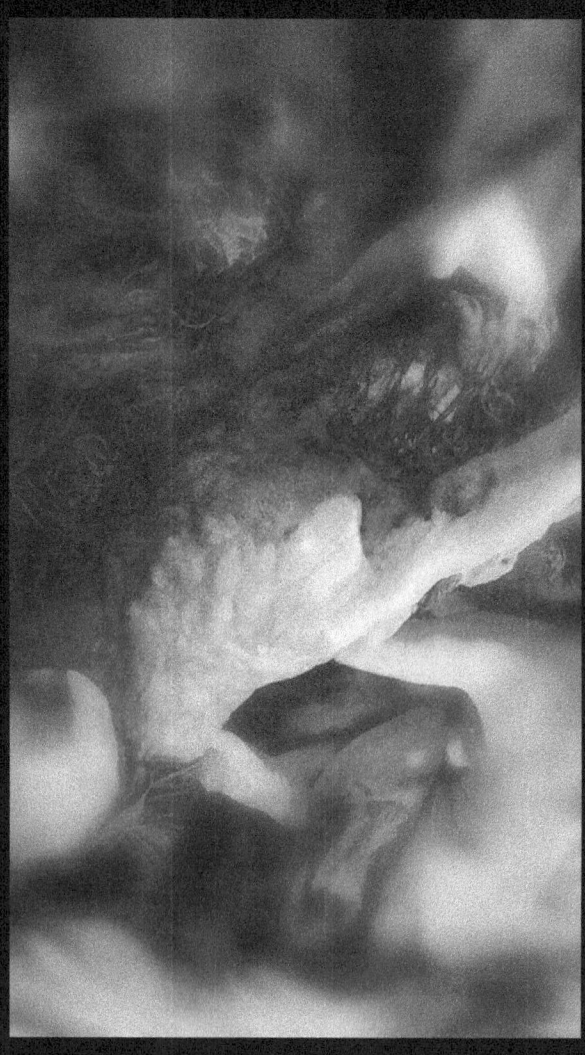

Journey of a Fallen Angel

"The blood they left me to die in, I drank it, I hexed it, my curses grew roots, my haunts outstretched forests...

I have often wondered why people underestimate the weak...
There are times, some of them grow monstrously dangerous."

~Channing M. The Monochrome of Darkness

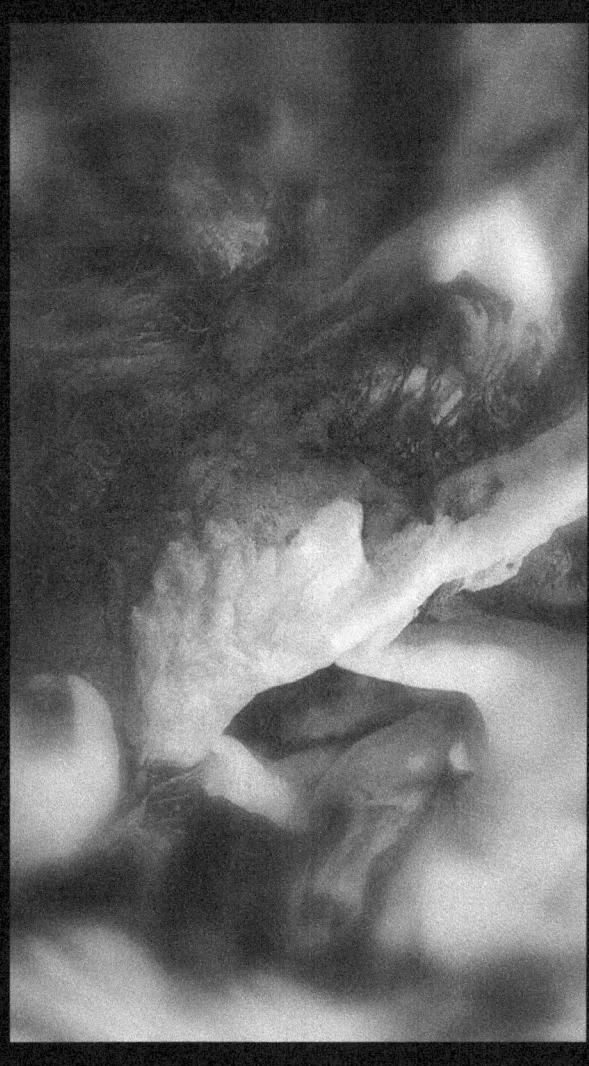

Journey of a Fallen Angel

"With lethargic eyes the poet stood;
deep wounds of his, lay armored,
unrelenting his fangs, scowling
thirst, unpitied, mournful- the
skies, vanished from his eyes...

his aching sight, his drest of love,
golden in blood, bathed in as the
night erased him from the winds."

~ Channing M. The
Monochrome of Darkness

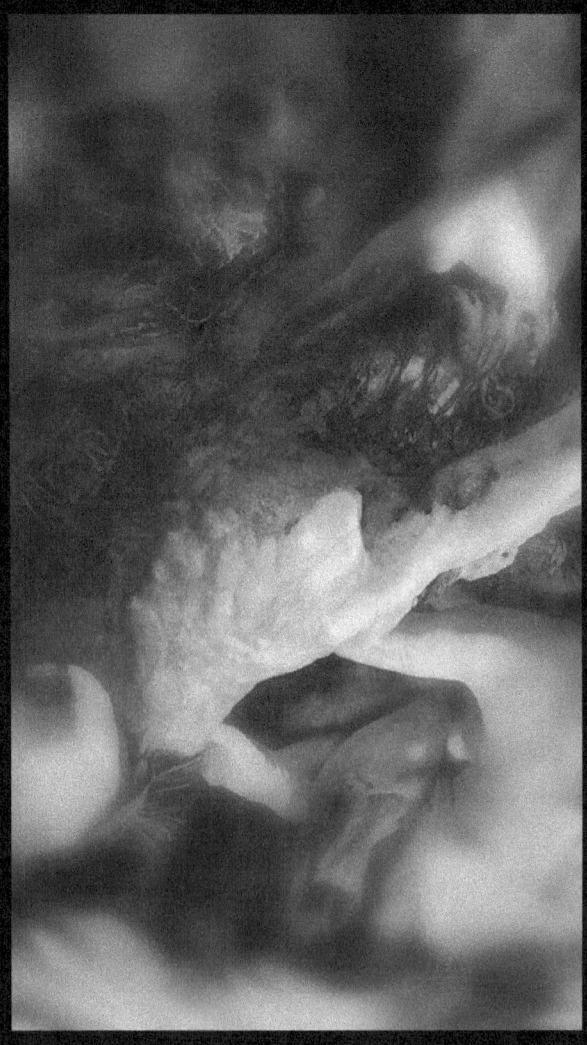

Journey of a Fallen Angel

"There was ardour in his footfalls, the ancient Chapels he walked in, the scaping vitriol in the greyness of hours, painting a dull, demented caparison, as if the slow dying winds howled for freedom, the cracks in stained glasses bled his soul, his silent eyes, cold and dead from the murderous presence of insanity, of grief, of decay. He was a spectacle of exorcism."

~Channing M, The Monochrome of Darkness

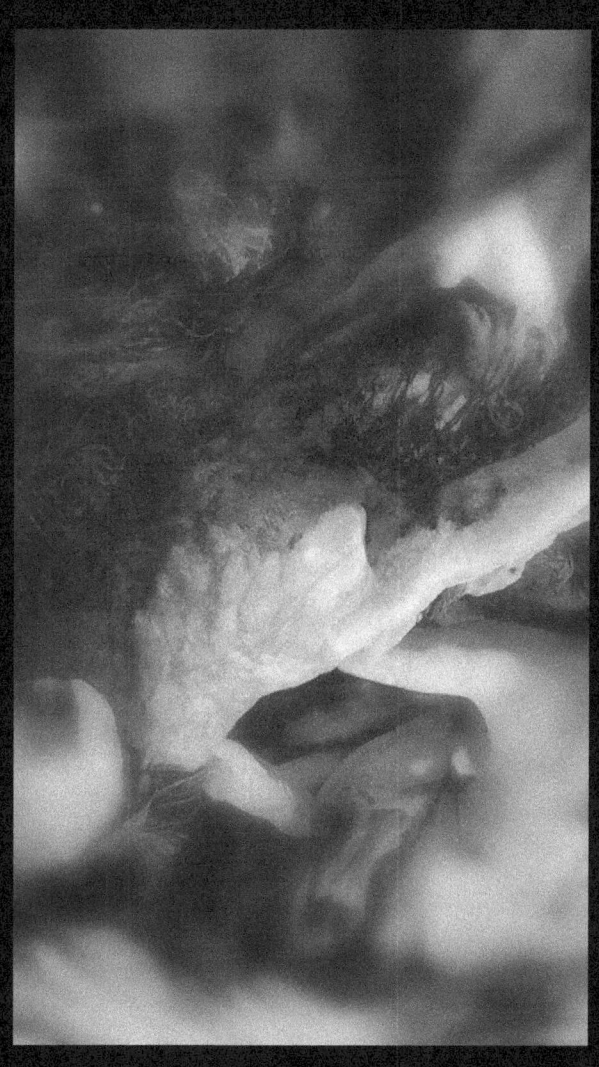

Journey of a Fallen Angel

"The spirit who inhibits him is me...
as if I draw his resonance to our words,
as if I am a language for him, a gorgeous fiend' who draws blood from his bleeding vein.
I am his haunt, I damn him, I am the God inside a Devil."

~Channing M, The Monochrome of Darkness

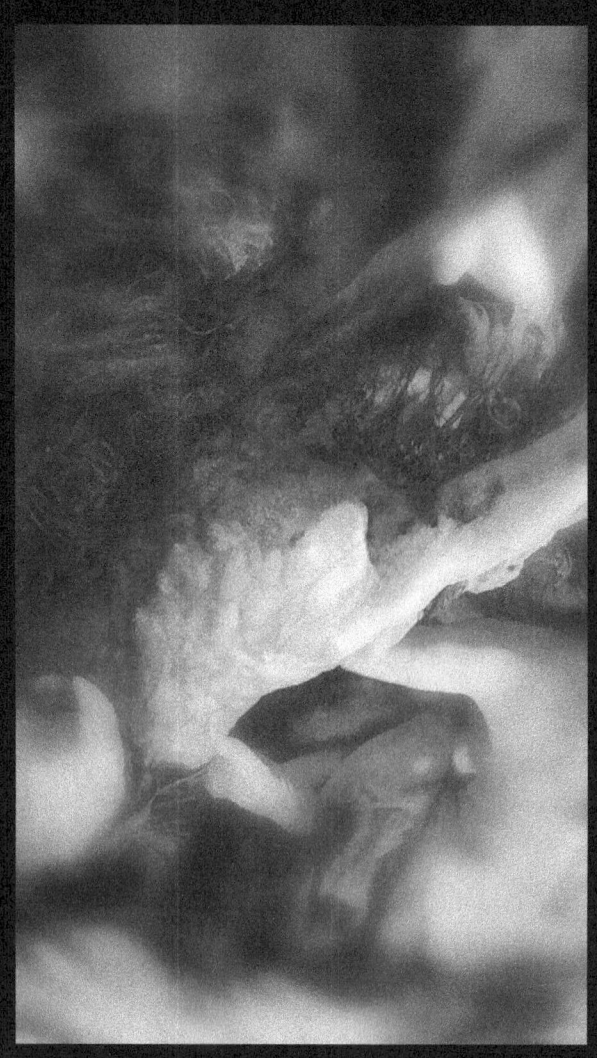

Journey of a Fallen Angel

"I couldn't reason if it was murder with intent or the contrary. If it was without intent, would it not have been an accident, as if I accidentally killed my soul in hapless withdrawal? If it was with intent, does' it not make me immune to any darkness?"

~Channing M. The Monochrome of Darkness

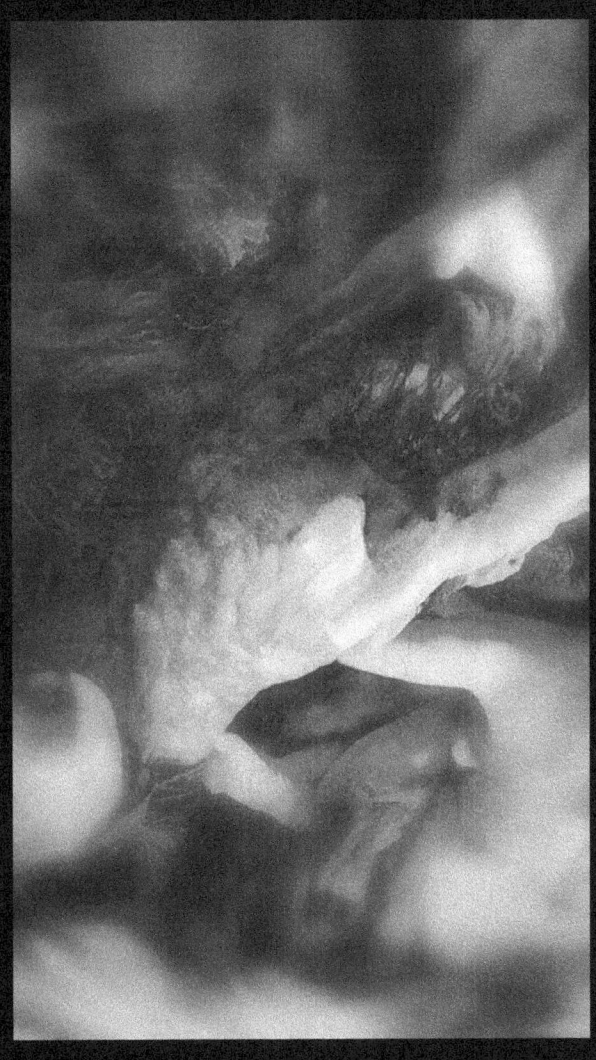

Journey of a Fallen Angel

"He was a frail sight to behold, so I crushed him in terrors. He wanted to build a castle of dreams and so I built him an inescapable prison. He wanted to soar high and love, and So I taught him to become the zenith and forget the weakness, tales can be written endlessly on how a monster survived, but not every light ends the darkness and I taught him not to survive, but to thrive."

~Channing M, The Monochrome of Darkness

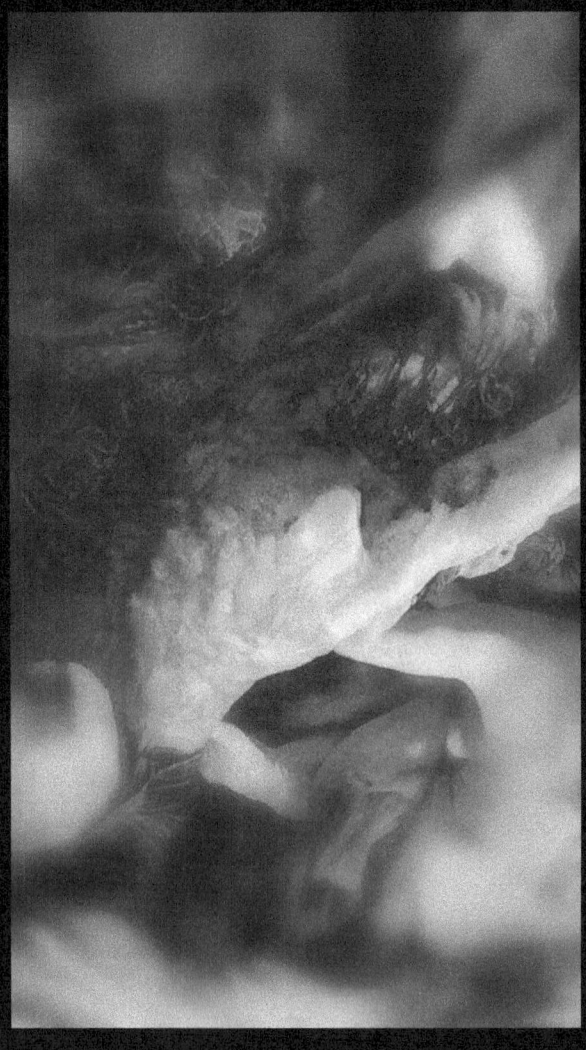

Journey of a Fallen Angel

"I fueled an art, sketched in sighs, its creases that full of scars, the paint had become moth-eaten, it looked as though it had a mind of its own, a decrepit heart that hungered blood, a painting that could blind the mortal eye, of a poet, bathed in blood, longing for an escape."

~Channing M. The Monochrome of Darkness

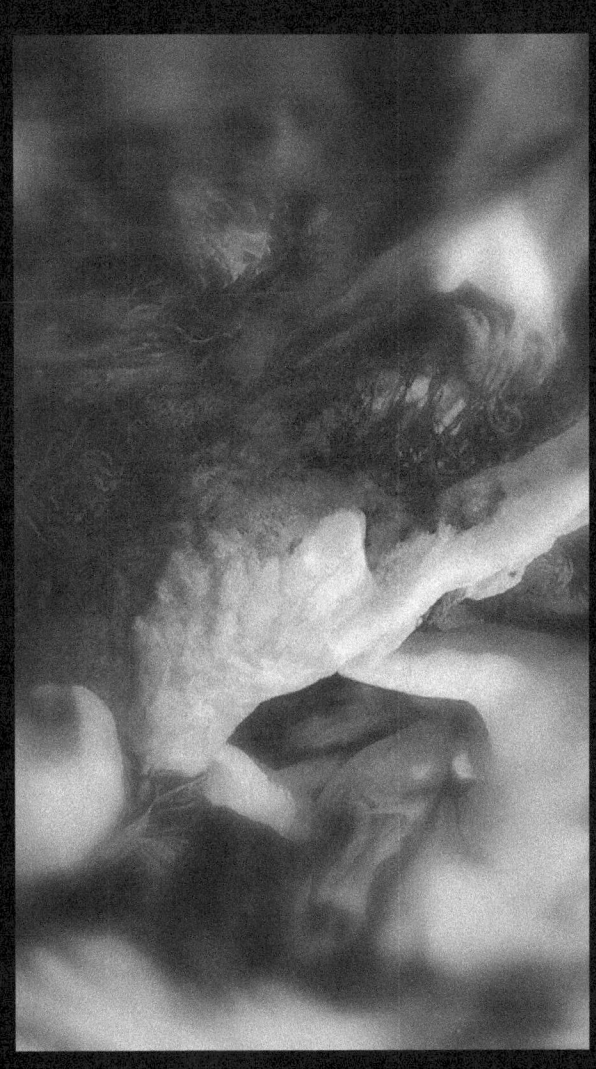

Journey of a Fallen Angel

"I was never meant for a Paradise, but this lascivious hunger, I have made hell, my heaven. As if I hold the world in this hourglass this minute knowing it's brokenness one day will remind me, stripping off all the heavens, I so dauntingly wear."

~Channing M, The Monochrome of Darkness

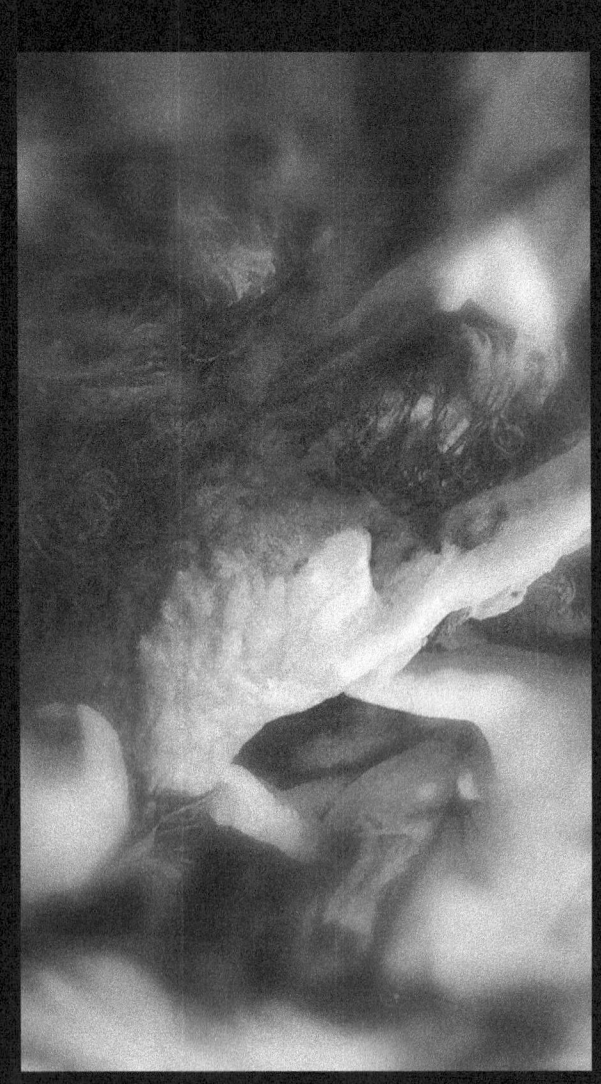

Journey of a Fallen Angel

"I wander as a ghost on ancient streets of Florence, my death unceremoniously done by the Misericordia, scraping the canvas of words, by the Arno River."

~Channing M. The Monochrome of Darkness

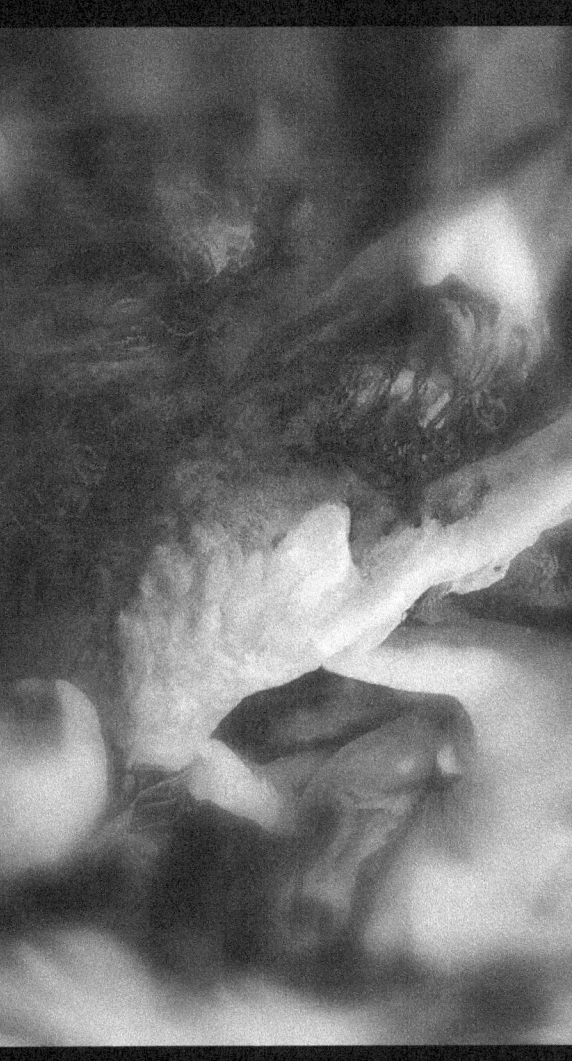

Journey of a Fallen Angel

"I was born of tainted blood and dark matter on a bridge of fire,

collapsing in the decay of its dust...

I was born of dirt, monstrous acts, and ruination of soul

and remained what came after was a dark matter of assonance.

Some say I came from nowhere, but that is exactly what I have

believed in, ridiculed for my disabilities, my shortcomings, I was an

easy prey for anyone at the spectacle.

I have risen from ashes of the dead, of winds of long past, left for decay

but I have expanded that darkness to resume a hemisphere of pride,

of stars, of galaxies. If I rose from being dead, I presumed,

was there any stoppage?

To those who die in these dearths, just like me.

Evolve if only for yourself. Evolve with rage and fire and ice.

Become an Iron fist. Become Iron. Become the sun. Become the Dark,

if only it keeps you alive.

Set afire the bridges that broke you, set afire the lands that hurt you,

set afire the souls that left you to rot.

I wish to those who are born from the stench of such abyss,

Lightening and Darkness and a wish that Blazing Fires fall short to

vanquish you.

I wish you Resurrection, And Rage, only to become invincible.

Only to survive hell."

~Channing M, The Monochrome of Darkness

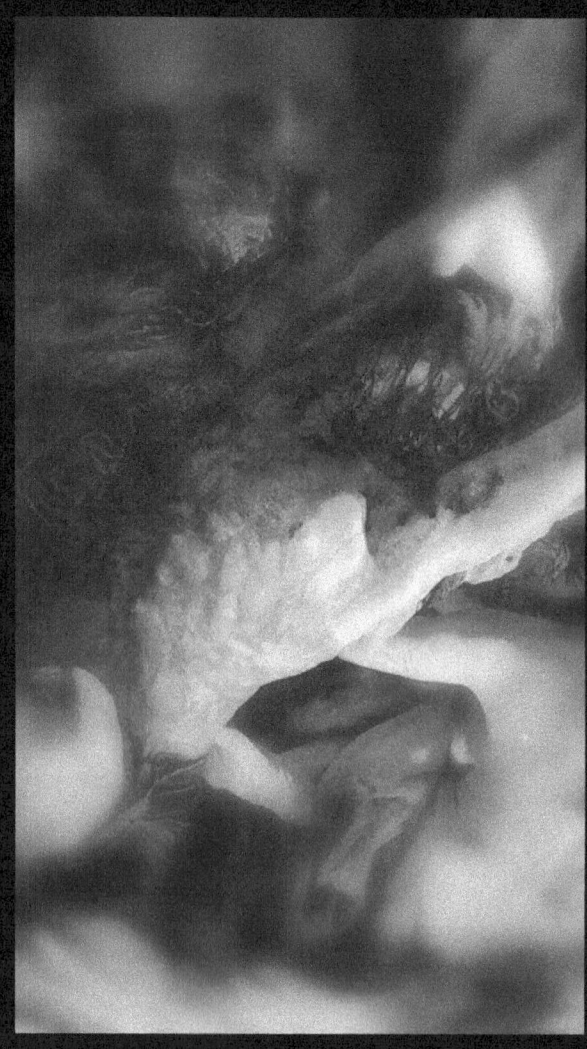

Journey of a Fallen Angel

"I buried a Poet in a grave of dusk, I embellished his skin with oleanders of the east, his breaths I wrapped dormant in seas of silk, his grey eyes I buried in his memories of stars.

as for the burning pyre that I burnt sending him across the lake, he burnt and burnt until the nights erased him in deathlike darkness."

~Channing M. The Monochrome of Darkness

Journey of a Fallen Angel

"Have you ever felt a melancholy so terrible that you know the way to your home but you don't? Your eyes can see but not really, your thoughts are so displaced, they seem lost. As if the soul itself has turned to ashes with an indescribable pain."

~Channing M, The Monochrome of Darkness

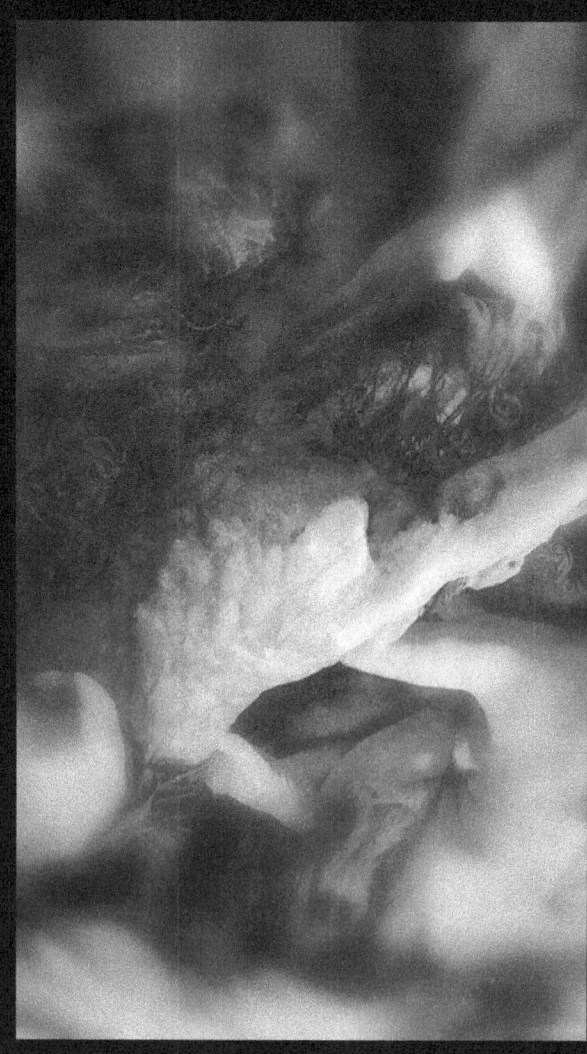

Journey of a Fallen Angel

"I walked my weary ways of grief, then time held it's dart on a selfless spree.

The words your mind hid, under the beatific sleeve, for my smiles that wandered across your ease, What journeys our hands held, yours in mine or mine changed? for skies are many that I painted black, but gazing upon you, the sun fell dark."

~Channing M, The Monochrome of Darkness

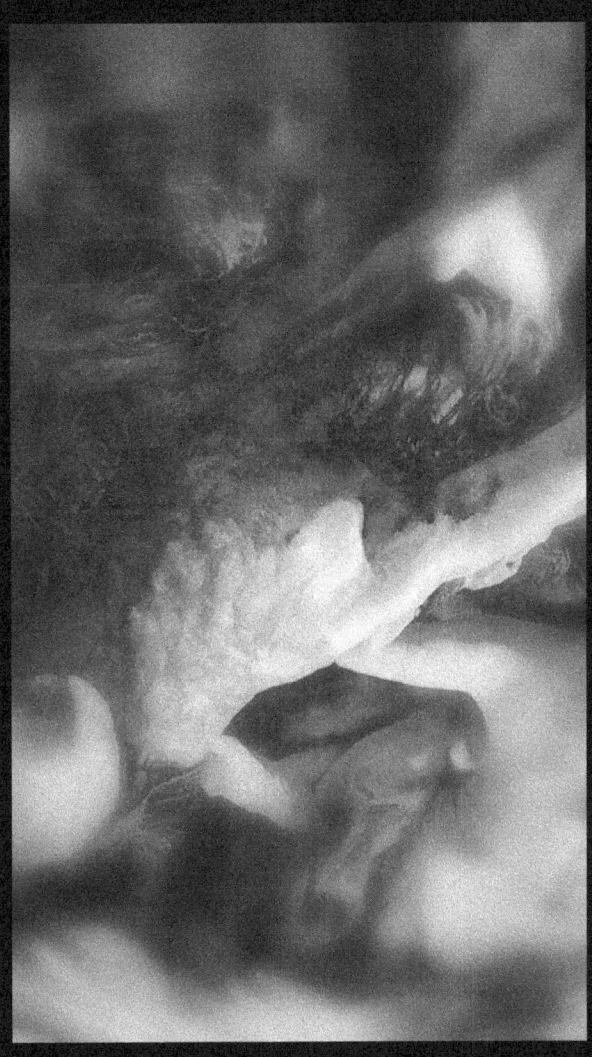

Journey of a Fallen Angel

"Came many monsters, to sign my death warrant, to have me rot how they claimed to create me, but below those vast skies of infinity, beyond the lighthouse of wisdom, I became a monster as I had to and nonetheless, I will stand alone if I have to, guarding the weight of endless graveyards in my heart."

~Channing M, The Monochrome of Darkness

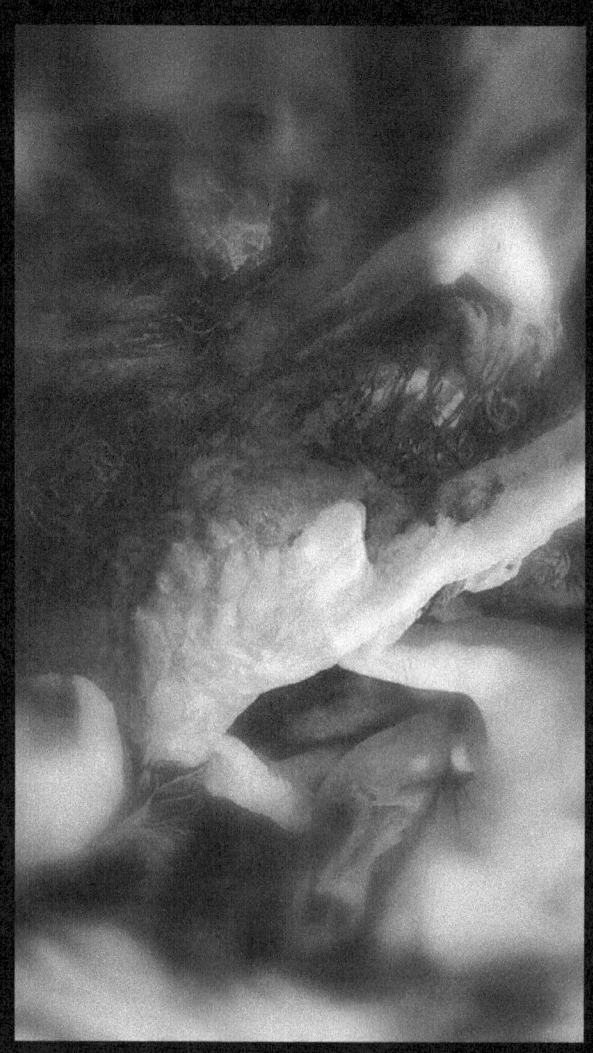

Journey of a Fallen Angel

"It is nightfall, and he walks in a garden of the graveyard, ghosted in roses, bloomed in the moonlight, befogged in moth laden scathes; divinely dead and yet alive in decay."

~Channing M, The Monochrome of Darkness

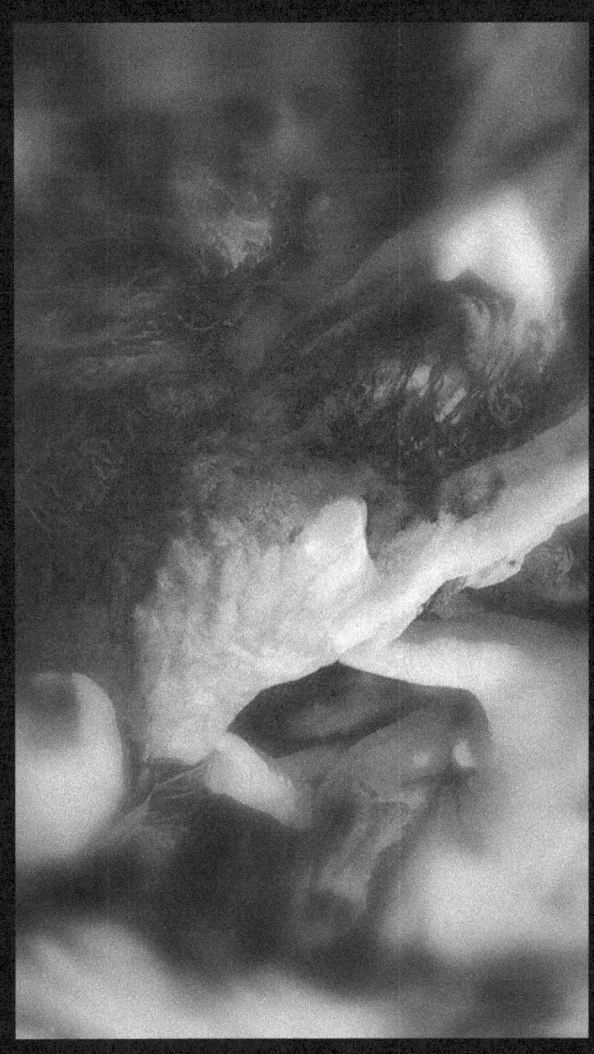

Journey of a Fallen Angel

"It is nightfall, and he walks in a garden of the graveyard, ghosted in roses, bloomed in the moonlight, befogged in moth laden scathes; divinely dead and yet alive in decay."

~Channing M. The Monochrome of Darkness

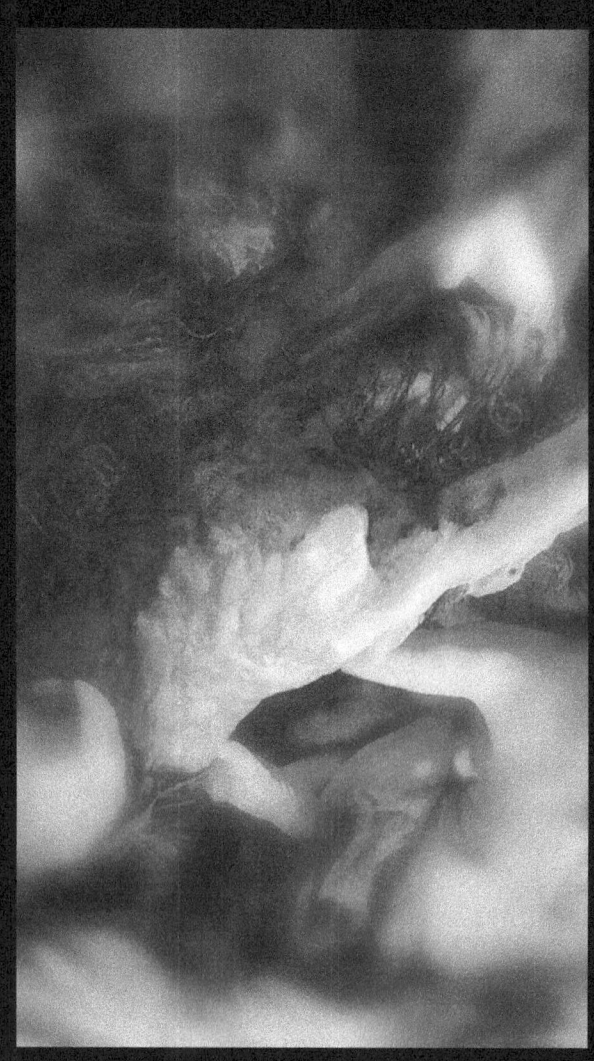

Journey of a Fallen Angel

"I have often wondered why I was painted in fragrances of romanticism, I should always have been painted in black blood and poetic cannibalism."

~Channing M, The Monochrome of Darkness

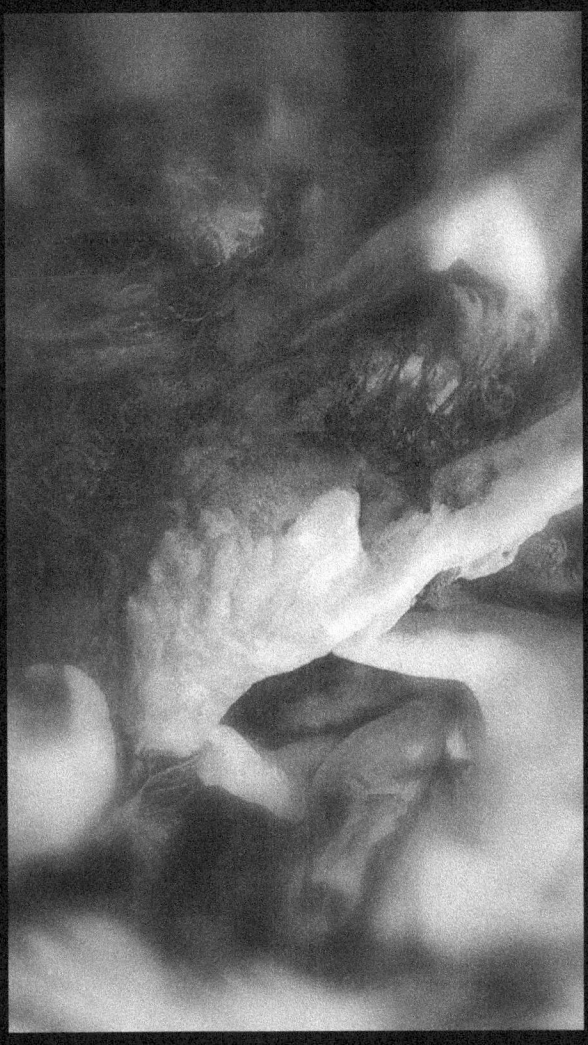

Journey of a Fallen Angel

"I have oft been asked what constructed a monster in me?

how does one curate it? how does one become it? Where I was concerned, an answer does exist within the marrow of horrors, it is plain in terms yet terse, I am not capable of forgiveness, nor am I capable of asking for it. The hurts that ever got inflicted on my skin, I never discarded it, I kept etching it in crevices, solidified it, so much so that it architectured a Palisade, it martyred every warmth within my skin, it cold pressed my mind into a significant horror. There, it is, the prologue of a pious monster, a heartless dreamer, and a ruthless annihilator."

~Channing M, The Monochrome of Darkness

Journey of a Fallen Angel

"I was never a candle which burned to give light to others and then burnt out. I was always a forest fire, I burn'd everything along with me."

~Channing M. The Monochrome of Darkness

Journey of a Fallen Angel

"There is something about early mornings that I spend smoking until the sun rises, it has oft served as a reminder, just like the ashes dropping from a burning cigarette, sometimes falling apart is better than being whole and feel nothing."

~Channing M, The Monochrome of Darkness

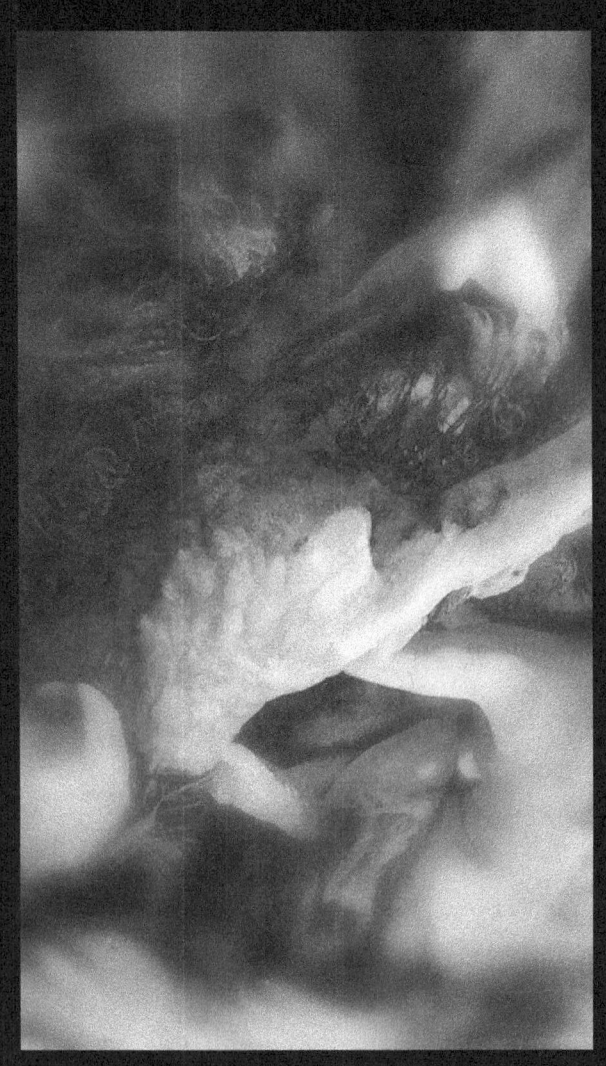

Journey of a Fallen Angel

"The monochrome winds panting on the stained windows of the Church, the howls of moon falling on the ground, dips a quill in blood and pens a macabre journey of a Fallen."

~Channing M. The Monochrome of Darkness

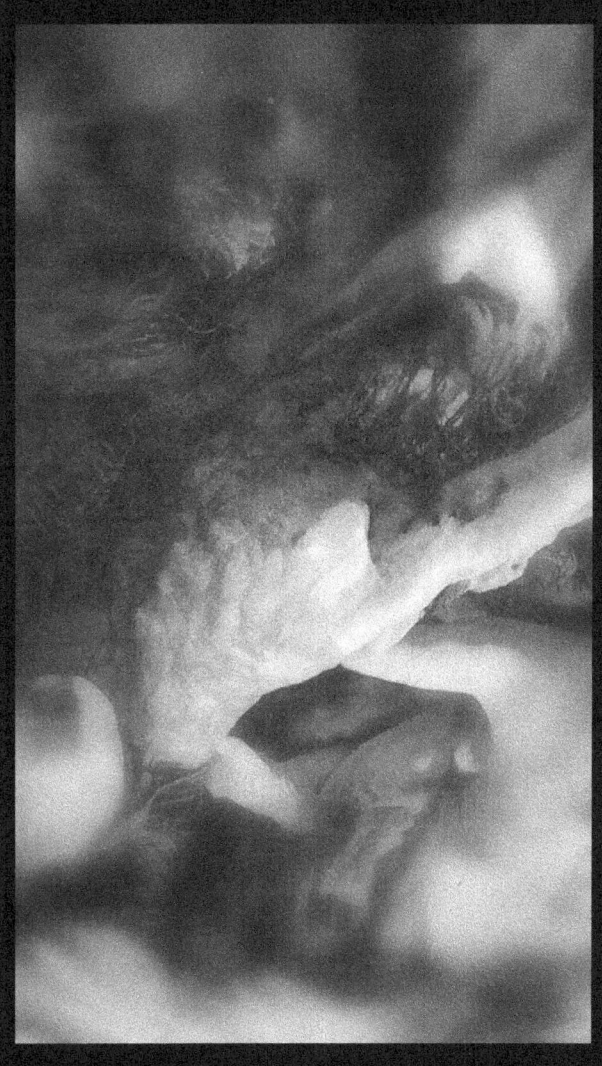

Journey of a Fallen Angel

"any happiness i have is borrowed
for, I am the unblessed,
the ruins of the abandoned..
for nature, nature will always win."

~Channing M, The Monochrome of Darkness

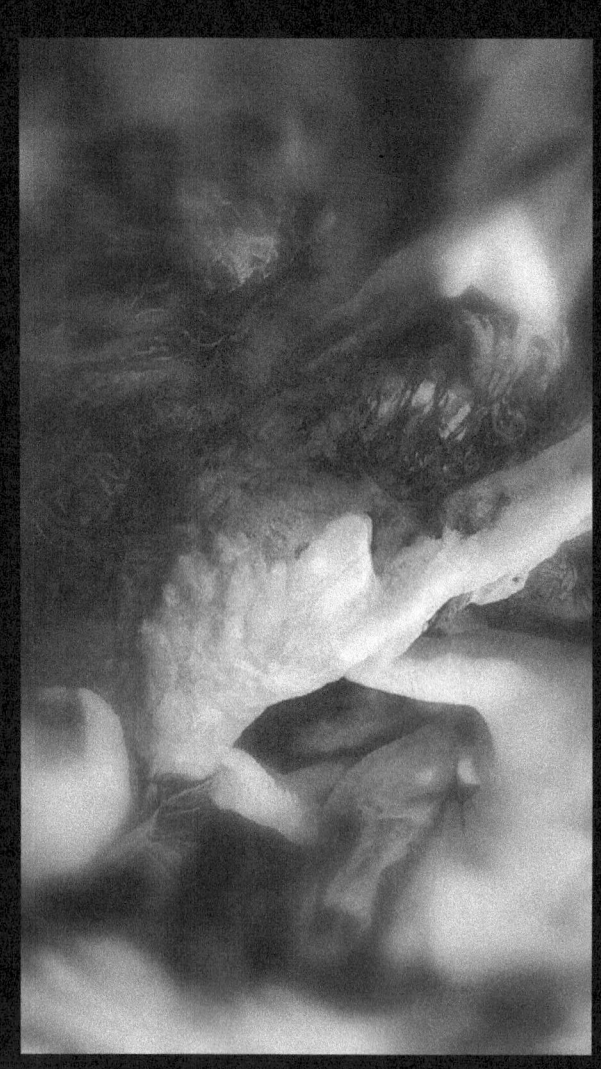

Journey of a Fallen Angel

"these bereaved winds,

on my window tonight,
are grieving the hauls of a forlorn
lover or a colossal debt? "

~Channing M. The
Monochrome of Darkness

The End

thank you for reading...

If you wish to reach me for any queries or wish to get in touch with me. Please feel free to write me

@: mcclarenc04@hotmail.com

www.ingramcontent.com/pod-product-compliance
Lightning Source LLC
Chambersburg PA
CBHW081255170426
43198CB00017B/2794